How the Maya
Built Their World

How the Maya Built Their World

Energetics and
Ancient Architecture

Elliot M. Abrams

UNIVERSITY OF TEXAS PRESS, AUSTIN

Copyright © 1994 by the University of Texas Press
All rights reserved
Printed in the United States of America
First edition, 1994

Requests for permission to reproduce material from this work should be sent to Permissions, University of Texas Press, Box 7819, Austin, TX 78713-7819.

⊗The paper used in this publication meets the minimum requirements of American National Standard for Information Sciences—Permanence of Paper for Printed Library Materials, ANSI Z39.48-1984.

Library of Congress Cataloging-in-Publication Data

Abrams, Elliot Marc, 1954–
    How the Maya built their world : energetics and ancient architecture / Elliot M. Abrams. — 1st ed.
        p.   cm.
    Includes bibliographical references and index.
    ISBN 0-292-70461-5 (cloth : alk. paper). — ISBN 0-292-70462-3 (pbk. : alk. paper)
        1. Copán Site (Honduras)   2. Mayas—Architecture.   3. Mayas—City planning.   4. Mayas—Antiquities.   5. Honduras—Antiquities.   6. Copán Site (Honduras)   I. Title.
    F1435.1.C7A26 1994
    338.4'769'00972838409021—dc20   93-47995

To my parents,
Doris and Herman Abrams

Contents

Figures

Tables

Preface

The ancient civilizations of the world constructed pyramids, temples, palaces, and other forms of public and private architecture that immediately capture our attention, appreciation, and wonderment. The architectural works built by the Maya civilization of Mexico and Central America are clearly recognized as some of the world's greatest architectural achievements. These architectural works are particularly impressive given the fact that they were built with the simplest of stone and wooden tools, powered exclusively by the strength of humans, and often in the midst of the wet tropical forest. If architecture symbolizes the challenge of humans against nature, then the ancient Maya were clear victors in a difficult struggle.

The great challenge of anthropological archaeology is to reconstruct as completely as possible cultural institutions, behaviors, and ideas from the archaeological materials of the past. The architectural remains represent one of the most durable, conspicuous, and culture-laden artifacts available to archaeologists, and the present study exemplifies one approach to the study of ancient architecture.

In this book I offer a description, methodology, and application of architectural energetics, which involves the translation of architecture into its energy equivalent. By converting buildings into the energy and labor expended in their construction, a series of reconstructions concerning social power, labor organization, and economics can be generated. This study of architectural energetics is applied to residential architecture at the Classic Maya center of Copan, Honduras; however, the book is intended to present and analytically justify this quantified approach to architectural studies such that further research, expanding beyond both the Maya region and residential architecture, may continue. I view the present study as an exploration of architectural energetics, illustrative but in no way exhaustive of the potential applications and refinements of architectural energetics.

One intriguing and perhaps dominant aspect of architecture at any large archaeological site is that the scale and quality of these structures have a profound impression on the observer. Archaeologists, from the moment we enter a site until the final analyses of data, are ultimately observers and interpreters of those observations. The leitmotiv of this volume is that the initial observation of large architectural accomplishments has a tremendous impact on our impressions and interpretations, just as the elite who commissioned such projects had originally intended.

As with any artifact within the material culture, this book too is the product of many contributions from various individuals. I would first like to thank the Instituto Hondureño de Antropología e Historia for providing authorization, support, and encouragement for my research. Special thanks are extended to the current executive director, José Maria Casco, as well as to Victor Cruz, Vito Veliz, and Oscar Cruz.

I would further like to thank the Dean's Office of the College of Arts and Sciences, Ohio University, for granting me two separate leave opportunities during which time much of the book was written.

A large number of scholars have contributed insights, data, and encouragement during the many years of research, analysis, and actual writing. In this regard, I offer special thanks to William T. Sanders for including me in the Proyecto Arqueológico Copán, Fase II, and for providing intellectual guidance in this and all of my anthropological research as well as to David Webster for his constant support, guidance, and friendship in the field and beyond.

I would also like to extend my thanks to those who provided insights, concern, and support while working in Copan: Charlie Cheek, Jack Mallory, Mary Spink, Jim Sheehy, Ricardo Agurcia, Ann Dowd, William Fash, Barbara Fash, Rene Viel, Rudy Larios, Susan Evans, Melissa Diamanti, Dave Rue, Stephen Whittington, Joe Guiliano, and Tom Sussenbach. My sincere thanks go to Arturo Sandoval and our Honduran field-workers, especially to those men who participated in the replicative experiments.

Other individuals who contributed in various ways and to whom I am grateful are Wendy Ashmore for her critical constructive reading of an earlier version of the manuscript, Nan Gonlin, Barbara Price, Gabriel Escobar, Jim

Hatch, Stephen Beckerman, David Shapiro, David Hyman, Stanley Loten, Dave Dabelko, David Slaw, Valerie Grimes, and one anonymous reviewer.

It is difficult to overstate how helpful Theresa J. May, University of Texas Press, has been. In fact, it was her invitation to write such a book that served as the catalyst for the refinement and expansion of my dissertation research. Without doubt, her encouragement and good spirits have been major factors in the completion of this book. I would also like to thank Carolyn Wylie and Alison Tartt for their work on the editing and production of the book. My thanks also to Peggy Sattler, Lisa Slates, Lars Lutton, and Rich Dickin of Ohio University for their work on the figures and photographs.

Finally, I would like to thank my wife, AnnCorinne Freter. It truly is impossible to specify all of her contributions, both as a friend and archaeologist, to this project. Needless to say, this book could not have been written without her. To Ann, Zach, Barry, Mitch, Ilene, and all of the other people who have helped me along the way, my heartfelt thanks.

How the Maya
Built Their World

1

Introduction

The very nature of the investigation of the archaeological remains of architecture changed dramatically with the embracing of an anthropological perspective (Willey and Sabloff 1980). Beginning and maturing in the decades of the 1960s and 1970s, the study of architecture evolved from one that emphasized the descriptive elements of architecture or the historic association of palatial and funerary architecture to one that viewed architecture as a consequence of ongoing social processes. As such, the anthropological perspective challenges the archaeologist to derive social and evolutionary meaning from the ruins of past societies.

The initial analyses of architecture understandably exhibited the wide range of directions that one would expect with the emergence and then growth of the new anthropological paradigm that was shaping archaeology. Settlement surveys relied upon architectural remains to generate and test models of urbanization (Willey 1956). Ancient public mounds built by egalitarian societies were viewed as demarcators of territorial and proprietary rights (Renfrew 1973). The energy expended in monumental construction was estimated to reveal the scale of sociopolitical complexity within a general ethnological taxonomy (Erasmus 1965).

In the decades following these pioneering studies, a large corpus of literature has grown concerning the anthropological analysis of architecture (see summaries in Abrams 1989; Lawrence and Low 1990; Kent 1990). The present study is designed to follow the logical continuum of one type of architectural analysis called *architectural energetics*. Architectural energetics involves the quantification of the cost of construction of architecture into a common unit of comparison—energy in the form of labor-time expenditure. Architecture, as a collection of raw and manufactured components, is translated into the composite cost of procuring and transporting those materials, manufacturing necessary parts, and assembling the finished product. This approach, as expressed in this book, is seen less as a replacement of other methodologies than as an exploration of the potential that this analysis may hold for anthropological archaeology.

To explore the effectiveness of such an approach, a specific site from which rather detailed architectural data are available is studied. Based on the enormous amount of available architectural data, the Maya site of Copan, Honduras, was chosen. The fact that the analysis must necessarily be site-specific will presumably not restrict its future application to sites outside the southern Maya lowlands.

Early Assessments of Maya Architecture

The lowland Maya Indians created one of the most complex cultural systems in a wet tropical environment in the New World (Figure 1), the study of which has attracted and fascinated scholars for over a century. The earliest archaeological investigations of the lowland Maya often focused on observations and interpretations concerning architectural achievements, principally based on qualitative assessments of scale and ornamentation. From the onset of the "discovery" of Maya centers, architecture was the most immediate and conspicuous form of evidence of the complexity, power, and splendor of the Maya civilization. Bishop de Landa, who provided the primary ethnohistoric description of the sixteenth-century Yucatecan Maya, referred to their architectural works as "the most remarkable of all the things which up to this day have been discovered in the Indies," adding that the sight of these buildings "fills one with astonishment" (Tozzer 1941:141). John L. Stephens (1841), the first popular Western chronicler of the ancient ruins of the southern lowland Maya centers, concluded that the prehispanic Maya must have built great urban centers, based on his impression of the beauty and enormity of the architectural ruins. These and other initial assessments of Maya architecture were perhaps in part influenced by the fact that the environmental setting of many of these ruins was the wet tropical forest, adding an element of mystery and accomplishment to the Maya, and that the comparative framework for observing Maya architecture was that of the classical civilizations of Egypt, Greece, and Rome. Since Maya architecture was per-

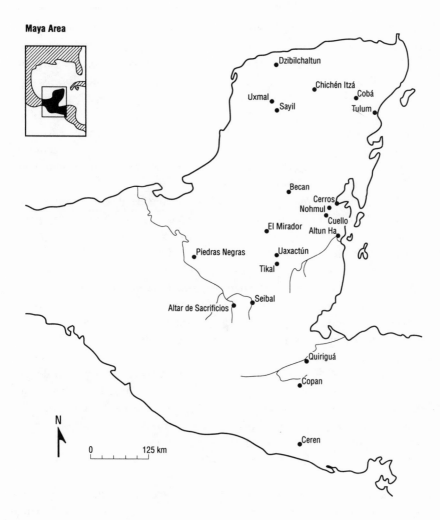

Maya Area

Dzibilchaltun

Chichén Itzá
Cobá
Uxmal
Sayil
Tulum

Becan
Cerros
Nohmul
Cuello
El Mirador
Altun Ha
Piedras Negras
Uaxactún
Tikal
Seibal
Altar de Sacrificios

Quiriguá
Copan

N

0   125 km

Ceren

Figure 1. The Maya lowlands

ceived as similar in scale, these Old World cultures, by inference, were deemed comparable (Totten 1926).

The analytic potential of Maya architecture was recognized very early in anthropology by Lewis Henry Morgan when he stated, "When rightly understood, they [Maya architectural accomplishments] will enable us to estimate the extent of the progress actually made, which was truly remarkable for a people still in barbarism, and no further advanced than the Middle Status" (1881:288). Although we neither use Morgan's terms nor endorse his explanations of the cultural evolutionary process, his observation noting the analytic import of architecture remains relevant.

Historically, Mayan archaeology has placed considerable attention on excavating the largest of architectural works from various sites; contemporary archaeologists are indebted to the pioneering efforts of the Peabody Museum and the Carnegie Institution, whose archaeological projects resulted in architectural reports that still represent some of the most detailed in Maya studies (Ashmore and Willey 1981). Nonetheless, the interpretations of the ancient Maya based on the analysis of architecture often relied upon subjective assessments of scale and quality of those structures. The assertion that the Maya did achieve a level of complexity associated with "civilization" has long been attributed to an impressionistic measure of size and elaboration of architecture (e.g., Childe 1950). The assessment of enormity of scale led A. V. Kidder, with reference to the architecture of Uaxactun, to infer that "it almost seems as if construction was conceived to be in itself an act of piety" (1950:12). This mentalistic evaluation of the Maya shared a place with similar monolithic psychological projections of obsession with time, calendrics, introversion, and ritual. Similarly, the qualitative assessment of the magnitude of architectural construction influenced J. Eric Thompson (1954) to directly implicate overtaxation of labor expended in elite construction projects in the presumed sudden and catastrophic collapse of the Maya state. Interestingly, even the concept of cultural "collapse" derives from the architectural or structural metaphor, evidence of the inculcation that architecture has had on our interpretation of the prehispanic Maya. More recently, George Andrews (1975:17) has continued this impressionistic assessment of Maya architecture by stating that only a particularly complex sociopolitical organization could "take on the herculean task of continuously rebuilding and extending the man-made domain."

The point of this brief overview is not to deny that the Maya built large and numerous structures or to minimize the outstanding pioneering descriptive research on architecture that has dominated Maya archaeology. Rather, it is intended to point out that interpretive statements concerning the ancient Maya have historically been based on subjective assessments rather than more empirical, quantitative studies of architectural scale. These subjective assessments consistently emphasize the extreme power and strength of rulers, reflected in their architectural projects. Ironically, this impression is exactly what the elite, when commissioning the construction of these edifices, wished to evoke from the Maya population; in a sense, the large architectural works serve as testament to the acute political skills of the Maya rulers.

Quantitative Assessments of Maya Architecture

It is considered essential for contemporary archaeologists to transcend subjective, qualitative assessments of architectural scale in reconstructing the Maya past. There have been two primary means through which architecture has been quantified in archaeological analysis. One means is based on a volumetric measure of architecture at a site or sites, with the comparative volumes serving as the basis of analysis. Various forms of volumetric quantification have been applied to the ancient Maya (Turner, Turner, and Adams 1981; Cheek 1986; Ringle and Andrews V 1988; Tourtellot 1988a). The principal goal of these studies has been to estimate relative political power and social status within a single site or among various sites.

The second means of quantification is an energetic assessment of architecture (Erasmus 1965; Arnold and Ford 1980; Folan et al. 1982; Abrams 1984a, 1987; Gonlin 1985, 1993; Ford 1991; Carmean 1991). This method involves, first, quantifying the volume of materials or components in architecture as in a volumetric study and, second, translating those volumes into their labor equivalence. The end result of this quantitative method is a labor cost estimate for each structure. As with the volumetric method, the analytic value of the energetic method lies in its applicability to comparative studies of power, status, and rank. It transcends the simpler volumetric method in providing the researcher with a more detailed and powerful measure of architecture, one that has not been fully exploited in Maya archaeology. In the present study, the energetic quantification of architecture, or architectural energetics, is detailed for the site of Copan, Honduras, with several applications offered to demonstrate the analytic value of this quantified method.

To the best of my knowledge, the earliest effort toward the energetic quantification of architecture was conducted at Chichen Itza (Morris, Charlot, and Morris 1931). During the restoration of the Temple of the Warriors, Earl Morris and his colleagues quantified in labor and time the cost of manufacturing and applying the plaster that at one time coated this large edifice.

This pioneering effort is somewhat tempered by their comment that "it is quite impossible to form an adequate conception of the amount of labor expended in construction of one of the ancient buildings" (ibid.:224).

The first major architectural energetic study, involving both methodology and analysis, was conducted by Charles Erasmus, who quantified civic architecture at Uxmal (1965). Combining volumetric measurements with labor costs based on replicative experiments, Erasmus was able to assess the level of complexity of this Maya center within Elman Service's (1962) taxonomy of sociopolitical types. Although Erasmus' interpretation was criticized (Sanders and Price 1968), his method was generally accepted. In addition, the costs generated through his replicative experiments have been applied in various other energetic studies, including my own work.

Overview of This Study

The relatively few quantified architectural studies—and explicitly energetic studies in particular—are countered by the majority of archaeological reports of the Classic Maya, which describe architecture in subjective terms such as "massive" and "huge." The lack of quantified research is ironic given that the analytic import of architecture among Mayanists is clearly recognized; Wendy Ashmore, for example, states that "the clearest indices of differential wealth at Quirigua would seem to be architectural—that is, the differential ability to commission monumental architecture and to incorporate masonry in construction" (1988:161).

The present volume provides a method of energetic quantification by which architectural scale and quality can be translated into the single analytic attribute of cost. To justify the energetic method, several applications of architectural energetics are presented for the Maya site of Copan, Honduras. The essential goal of the book is to show the value of architectural energetics as an important component to archaeological studies in anthropology. I hope that parallel studies at other sites, within and beyond the Maya region, will lead to the maturation of such studies.

In Chapter 2, the site of Copan, Honduras, is described in terms of environmental setting and the previous architectural research that is germane to the construction process. Although Copan is the focus of this analysis, many of the results of this single case are transferable to other Maya sites. Chapter 3 describes the various forms of Classic Maya residential architecture and considers the factors contributing to those forms. Although the method of quantification is applicable to any type of building, the analyses all focus on residential structures; thus Chapter 3 deals more with domestic rather than civic architecture. Although a wide range of factors are recognized as being instrumental in affecting residential form, I argue, following a materialist-selectionist perspective, that the consequences of form on the biopsycholog-ical quality of life take priority as "determinants" of one's mental conception of form. Establishing the idea that differential quality of life characterizes various residential forms is analytically important, for then domestic archi-tecture is linked behaviorally with status and power distinctions as well as with symbolic values assigned to architecture by the Classic Maya. The methodology of quantifying architecture into energy equivalence is detailed in Chapter 4, as is the description of the range of structures within my sample. The structures in my sample are all fully excavated and span the entire spectrum of statuses at Copan, from king to commoner, expanding beyond previous analyses. Chapter 5 presents additional behavioral aspects of construction, use, and maintenance of buildings, thus supplementing the more empirical aspects of the architecture per se. Chapter 6 begins the series of logical inferences derived from the energetic assessment of architectural scale and quality, focusing directly on reconstructing the sociopolitical hier-archy at Late Classic Copan—essentially an energetic refinement of settle-ment analysis. Chapter 7 combines this reconstruction with the energetic cost estimates to generate the organization of labor for the purpose of con-struction. Chapter 8 addresses the question of specialization of construction personnel within a broader model of the ancient Maya economy. The final chapter draws various conclusions about Maya archaeology and the study of architecture, emphasizing the need for expanding the energetic approach. To place this study in broader perspective, this last chapter discusses studies con-ducted elsewhere in the world as a means through which future comparative research can be assessed. Thus, although the book must necessarily focus on a single site, its application is arguably global.

Since data and analysis are of value only within the context of a broader theoretical framework, it is necessary to state that the orientation here is explicitly materialistic. The analyses focus on the comparison and interpre-tation of collective measures of architectural cost rather than on the more symbolic or psychologic dimensions of the architecture, although these fac-tors are in reality not disarticulated. One could perhaps deconstruct this ma-terialistic orientation to posit some deeper explanation for this decision. However, the more surficial explanation for selecting a materialist approach to scrutinize architecture is that it is methodologically accessible and repre-sents the most effective means of answering the questions posed within this research. Even with its flaws (as I discuss in Chapter 4), a quantitative approach to understanding behaviors associated with construction, or a comparison of costs and benefits of various architectural forms to best assess desirability of form, is preferred to many alternatives in that the method is explicit, replicable, and analogous to observable patterns of behavior in the contemporary world, as is discussed in Chapter 3. In essence, the approach taken here—that of architectural energetics—is considered "scientific," or at least more scientific than many alternatives (cf. Binford 1989). Some very interesting analyses of architecture are directed at such questions as style, perceptions of space, archaeoastronomy, and geomancy (e.g., Lawrence and Low 1990; Kent 1990). Nonetheless, the dimensions of architecture analyzed in these studies have little if any bearing on the *cost* of construction, and thus this book does not delve into these important yet quite distinct analyses.

2

Background to Architectural Energetics at Copan

The architectural data that are quantified in this study have been excavated at the Maya site of Copan, Honduras. I focus on this one site for various reasons. First, we have very detailed architectural data from this site, a consequence of the long history of excavation at Copan and the specific research design implemented by the Proyecto Arqueológico Copán, Fase II (PAC II), on which I worked in 1980 and 1981. Second, part of the total work of the PAC II involved very accurate reconstructions of the excavated structures, under the direction of Rudy Larios V., an outstanding architect and restorer of Maya buildings. This restoration allowed me to observe and collect data relating to the construction of architecture. Third, in addition to numerous previous analyses, a large number of analyses were to be conducted at Copan, and thus the energetic analysis at this specific site could then be applied to broader research.

Since the architecture from Copan will serve as the centerpiece of the ensuing analyses, a brief historic outline of archaeological research at the site, especially research involving architecture, is in order. The ensuing description is not meant to minimize the importance of nonarchitectural research, but rather to concentrate attention on the scope and types of data that are incorporated in the present analyses and thus are directly germane to meeting the goals of this book.

Architectural Research at Copan

Copan, Honduras, is one of the largest Maya centers in terms of architectural scale (Figures 2, 3, and 4). Its Main Group was initially mapped by John L.

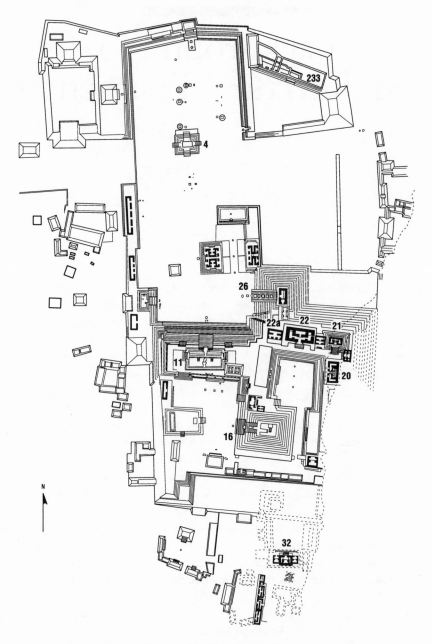

Figure 2. The Main Group, Copan
(from Webster 1989, with permission from Dumbarton Oaks and the author)

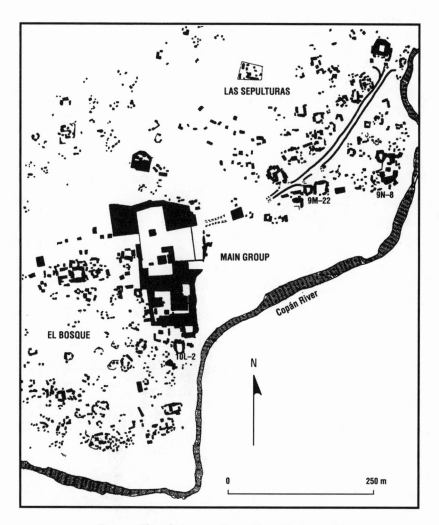

Figure 3. The urban zones, Copan (from Sheehy 1991)

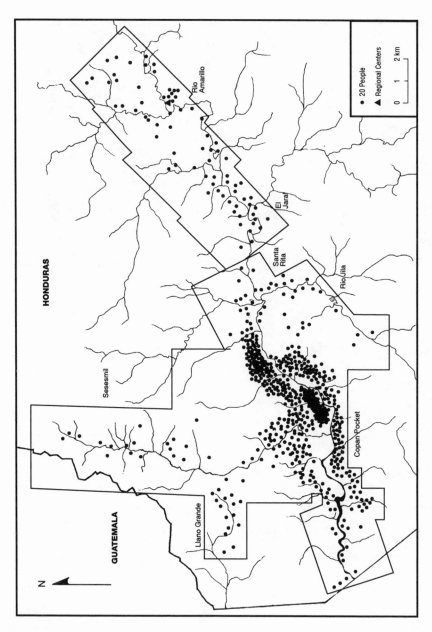

Figure 4. The distribution of the Late Classic population in the Copan Valley
(from Freter 1992, with permission from Cambridge University Press and the author)

Stephens (1841), and although this effort produced little more than a thoughtful sketch map, the major structures within the Main Group were located. The first major excavations at Copan, conducted and reported by Alfred Maudslay (1889–1902), focused upon some of these larger structures, including Structures 4, 11, 16, 20, and 22. These excavations were not extensive, consisting of the clearing and trenching of structures. Maudslay's contribution further included providing a map of the Main Group more accurate than that of Stephens as well as elevations of the Main Group, thus reducing confusion caused by the differential height of the Acropolis.

The next major project at Copan, sponsored by the Peabody Museum from 1891 to 1895, was conducted by George B. Gordon, John Owens, and Marshall Saville (Gordon 1896, 1902). In keeping with the research design of the times, it likewise focused effort on architecture within the Main Group. During this project, Structures 7, 9, 10, 11, 21, 21a, and 26 were excavated using both horizontal stripping and deep-trenching techniques. The Peabody effort also restored these structures to their present form. Owens noted that the *corte* profile—the stratigraphic profile of the East Court of the Acropolis exposed by erosion from the Copan River—revealed that three building episodes were responsible for producing the final Acropolis height. Sylvanus G. Morley (1920:8–9) suggested, however, that perhaps five or six distinct episodes of construction were evident. In addition to adding more structures to an increasingly accurate map of the Main Group, the first "house mound" at Copan was excavated under the direction of Gordon. Structure 36, located south of the Main Group, would currently be considered the residential structure of a rather high-ranking member of the elite and hardly in the category of a commoner's dwelling, the subject of Wauchope's (1934) housemound excavations at Uaxactun. Nonetheless, it does represent the first excavation of architecture outside the confines of the Main Group.

The Peabody research was followed by work sponsored by the Carnegie Institution of Washington, from 1935 to 1946 (excluding 1943–1945), under the direction of Gustav Stromsvik. The research design was again rather explicitly oriented toward the excavation of architecture in the Main Group. During this project, Structures 11 and 22, the Jaguar Stairway in the East Court, the Reviewing Stand in the West Court, the Hieroglyphic Stairway, and the Ball Court within the Great Plaza were either partially or completely excavated and restored (Trik 1939; Longyear 1952). It was during the Carnegie project that further architectural destruction of the East Court was prevented through the redirection of the Copan River. The project also produced the first settlement survey of architecture outside the Main Group, supplying preliminary data on the number and configuration of structures within the central 18 sq. km of the Copan pocket.

From 1975 to the present, a continuous series of projects has been conducted at Copan, all of which have involved excavation and mapping of architecture. From 1975 to 1978, Gordon Willey directed the Harvard project, which focused on mapping the cluster of courtyard units east of the Main Group, termed Las Sepulturas. In doing so, a hierarchic classification of structures and courtyards—based on size, number of structures, and presence or absence of vaulted stones—was produced (Leventhal 1979; also Willey, Leventhal, and Fash 1978; Willey and Leventhal 1979). This five-part classification, later expanded by Freter (1988; see Table 1), incorporated much of the range of variability in architecture, with Type 1 courtyards at

Table 1. PAC II Site Typology

Site Type	Description
Nonmound	Surface concentration of artifacts with no associated building debris
Single mound	Isolated mound
Aggregate mound	2–3 mounds with no formal courtyard; structures less than 1 m in height; earth or cobble construction
Type 1	3–5 mounds with 1 structure less than 1 m in height; cobble or masonry construction
Type 2	6–8 mounds with 1–2 courtyards; mounds less than 3 m in height; cobble or masonry construction
Type 3	6–10 mounds with 1–3 courtyards; mounds less than 5 m in height; some vaulted structures
Type 4	8–100 mounds with multiple courtyards; some mounds greater than 5 m in height; increased number of vaulted structures; sculpture
Type 5	Main Group complex

Source: Freter 1988; modified from Leventhal 1979.

the lower end and Type 4 courtyards at the upper end (the single Type 5 courtyard is represented by the Main Group). In addition, each of the courtyard units was given a "CV" (Copan Valley) number, and CV's 16, 20, 43, 45, 46, and 47 were cleared, partially excavated, or trenched for earlier structures. This project was pivotal in its elucidation of architectural variability, since structures outside the Main Group received comparable archaeological attention, a prerequisite for any comparative analysis of the cost differentials of architecture and the social relations reflected by those costs. Interestingly, as attention was being directed outside the Main Group by archaeologists, architects were mapping in great detail all of the structures in the Main Group (Hohmann and Vogrin 1982).

Proyecto Arqueológico Copán, Fase I (PAC I), immediately followed and expanded upon the work begun by the Harvard Project. Directed by Claude Baudez from 1978 to 1980, this project designed a series of research questions diverse in character yet convergent in their focus of expanding upon previous projects. Again focusing the present discussion on the recovery of architectural data, PAC I completely excavated Structures 4 and 18 in the Main Group; mapped the clusters of courtyards in the El Bosque barrio, an urban zone for persons of subroyal status located west and south of the Main Group; and excavated a small ball court in the El Bosque zone (Baudez 1983). In addition, deep trenching was conducted in the Great Plaza and the East Court, increasing our understanding of the construction history in these areas (Cheek 1983, 1986; Becker 1983). Cheek's (1986) analysis of the comparative basal volumes of architecture in the Great Plaza represents the first and only volumetric study of architecture through time at any Maya site. Finally, two settlement surveys were conducted (Fash 1983; Vlcek and Fash 1986). The continuity between this and previous projects is most strikingly illustrated by the fact that the excavation of Structure 4, which Maudslay began in 1885, was completed nearly one hundred years later.

The second phase of the project, PAC II, was directed by William Sanders and David Webster and ran from 1980 to 1984. Although one structure— Structure 233 on Platform 3—within the Main Group was excavated (Cheek and Spink 1986), the vast majority of effort was directed at complete horizontal excavation and trenching of structures located within the Las Sepulturas barrio (Sanders 1986a, 1990). Most of the structures within the Type IV unit (designated 9N-8) were excavated, adding tremendous architectural data concerning statuses below that of a ruler yet above that of the commoner. The focus on horizontal exposure resulted in data for the complete final structure, making possible the volumetric assessment of various buildings, one essential component to the energetic methodology used in the present analysis.

Subsequent projects have focused on the settlement both within and beyond the main urban concentrations (Webster and Freter 1990a, 1990b; Webster and Gonlin 1988; Freter 1988, 1992; Ashmore 1991; Gonlin 1993), and excavations continue in the Main Group. The Copan Mosaics Project, beginning in 1985 under the direction of William Fash, undertook the reassembly of sculptural blocks from the Main Group. Beginning in 1988, under the joint direction of William Fash, Robert Sharer, E. Wyllys Andrews V, Ricardo Agurcia, Barbara Fash, and Rudy Larios, the Proyecto Arqueológico Acropolis de Copán (PAAC) has recovered very important data from the Main Group—specifically Structures 10L-26, 16, and the East Court—and from Group 10L-2 (Fash 1991a; Fash and Stuart 1991; W. Fash et al. 1992; Sharer, Miller, and Traxler 1992; Andrews V and Fash 1992; B. Fash et al. 1992). This cumulative research makes Copan perhaps the most archaeologically investigated southern lowland Maya site and certainly provides an enviable corpus of architectural data that serves as the foundation for the present study and a springboard for comparative analyses.

Environment of the Copan Valley

Since architecture is ultimately a collection of modified and unmodified raw materials, the key resources necessary for construction within the Copan Valley must be described. Researchers conducting parallel studies of architecture and construction at other Maya sites should bear in mind the specific environmental constraints and incentives associated with those sites.

Copan is the largest Maya site in the southeast periphery of the Maya lowlands, located about 14 km from the Guatemalan border in Honduras. The Copan River is the dominant environmental feature in terms of geomorphology and vital resources that attracted settlers at various times (Figure 5). The Copan River flows in a westerly direction until it joins with the Motagua River in Guatamala, which in turn flows into the Caribbean Sea. In addition to being an essential resource for sustaining human life, the river also supplied water used in construction and was a conduit through which various stones, in the form of cobbles, could be readily obtained for construction. In conjunction with the constriction of the flanking hills, the Copan River also produced relatively deep alluvial soils in pockets that were the primary agronomic resource to the Copan Maya. Many of these soils were also central to the construction process, since earth was the principal raw material in

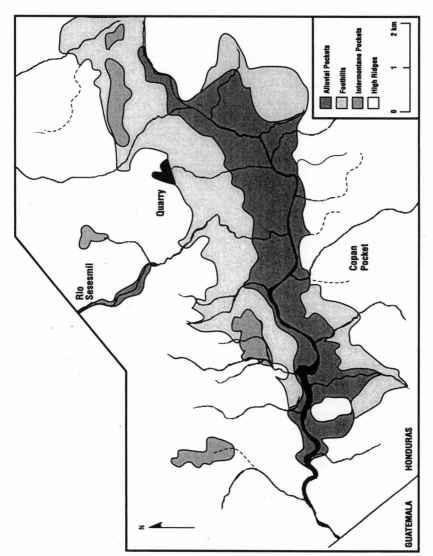

Figure 5. Copan environmental zones

construction fill, and earth mixed with water served as mortar in masonry constructions. Although borrow pits—the remnant pits of excavated earth— have not yet been systematically tested archaeologically, the PAC II rural settlement surveys and the Copan pocket survey did record depressions on the landscape adjacent to clusters of settlement, and these depressions may have been such borrow pits.

The flanking foothill and mountain ecozones provided a range of natural resources exploited for construction, the first and foremost being tuff. Tuff is an igneous stone that dominates the northern flanking mountainous zone (Turner et al. 1983:56), and virtually every masonry structure and stela was produced from this raw material. This is in contrast to most other lowland sites, which used limestone as the dominant stone for construction (Pollock 1965). The Copanecos, however, lost nothing by relying upon tuff; as Morley wrote (1920:6), "Its excellent qualities are in no small part responsible for the remarkable plastic art which developed here." A large quarry located approximately 1 km north of the Main Group has long been known (Morley 1920:6; see also Figure 5); in fact, a huge section of the mountain just west of that quarry appears to have been removed by the ancient Copanecos. Untapped reservoirs of tuff in the northern mountains still remain. In my own quarrying experiments conducted in 1981, I had no trouble finding an outcrop of tuff just upstream from the Sesesmil tributary. A return to that same quarry in 1990 found it nearly undisturbed and still loaded with tuff. Apparently Morley's observation (1920:5) that there are "unlimited quantities of excellent building materials in the immediate vicinity of the ruins" appears as correct today as it was in 1920.

The mountain zone is also the source of limestone used in the manufacture of plaster, as well as various amorphous silicas and igneous stones that erode from the mountains and flow eventually into the Copan River through a series of streams, or *quebradas*. In addition, the upland zone is a source of wood, the dominant raw material in commoner structures; although wood was limited in masonry structures, beams, arch supports, and lintels were made exclusively from it. Undoubtedly, these components of masonry structures required hardwoods; the lintel of Structure 10L-22A was manufactured from one known hardwood species (*chicozapote;* B. Fash et al. 1992), and other hardwood species have recently been identified at the site (Lentz 1991:279). With reference to commoner residences, I interviewed several Copanecos concerning the tree species used today. I was told that seventeen tree and four vine species were used in wattle and daub house construction, including both hardwoods and softwoods of various sizes (Abrams

1984a:148). Of these, pine (*Pinus oocarpus*) was the most relied upon species due to its abundance, availability, and ease in cutting a range of thicknesses, making it suitable for all components of the house. Recent analyses have confirmed that pine was both abundant in the natural ecosystem of the Classic period (Rue 1987) and predominant as a raw material in house construction (Lentz 1991). Although pine can be used as any component of the house, informants revealed that hardwoods, if available, are preferred for the mainposts, or corner supporting posts, of the house.

The final raw material found within the Copan Valley necessary for construction is vegetation for roofing. Several lines of evidence indicate that roofing material by and large was probably a local grass called *zacate paraguas*. Although Morley (1920:3) suggested that palm thatch served as the roofing material and Stephens (1841:109) observed blades of corn husks serving as an adequate roofing material, several factors suggest that thinner grass was the most likely material for this purpose. Grass is local and abundant, growing on both the alluvial soils and the foothills, and is thus inexpensive and readily available. Today it is the dominant organic material used in roofing. By contrast, the closest source of palm thatch viable for roofing today is about 25 km outside of Copan. Although two species of palm have recently been identified to have existed at Late Classic Copan (Lentz 1991), neither is desired as a roofing material today, and I will assume that they were similarly eschewed as a roofing material in the past. Differential cost efficiencies are strong influences on decision making, whether by ancient or contemporary people, and can thus be used as the basis for inferring past instituted behaviors. This principle is expanded upon in the following chapter in the context of the description and comparison of residential architecture of the Classic Maya.

3

Maya Architectural Forms

Any analysis of Maya architecture requires a description and classification of the variety of forms within that artifact category. Architectural form is created through a very complex interplay of decisions based on preexisting concepts of form that are influenced by external material concerns within a context of cultural history (Oliver 1987). As such, it is a subject that has been addressed in Maya archaeology through various descriptive and theoretical positions. Analyses have ranged from the art historic (Schele and Miller 1986) to the mechanical (Roys 1934); from geomancy and settlements (Ashmore 1986, 1991) to geology and sediments (Bullard 1960); from dwellings of commoners (Webster and Gonlin 1988) to those of royalty (Proskouriakoff 1946). Given, then, the breadth of analyses and thus the potential classificatory schemes, it must be made clear that the description of architectural forms presented in this chapter is most profoundly influenced by the comparative energetic costs of construction. In a strict sense, no taxonomy is necessary since all architecture is reduced to the single continuous variable of cost; nonetheless, heuristic considerations require classification.

For the purpose of discussion, and guided by the analyses that follow, this chapter will consider only residential structures, classified into two very elemental and distinct forms: the basic form and the improved form. At Copan the basic form refers to wattle and daub residences built on low platforms; available data from extensive settlement and excavation studies (Freter 1988; Webster and Gonlin 1988) suggest that platformless residences, found at other Maya sites like Cuello (Wilk and Wilhite 1991) and Nohmul (Pyburn

1990), were not built at Copan. The improved form refers to any residence significantly more costly than the basic form, the key diagnostic at Copan being the presence of masonry superstructure walls. Theoretical questions are then considered in terms of how one analyzes form. Following this, these two general house types are contrasted, less in terms of the origins or creation of form than in terms of the material costs and benefits that these two house types provided to their respective occupants. The material consequences of housing are suggested as the more profound selective agents influencing the evolution of form. I focus exclusively on residential structures in this particular discussion since the residence represents that microenvironment which, perhaps more than any other, affects the quality of life and thus the behavioral and psychological condition of individuals.

As with any artifact, the description and categorization of architecture is ultimately fashioned to best suit the specific analysis. However, the breadth of articulation between numerous behaviors and thoughts makes any single definition of architecture difficult. The problem of simply defining the house, for example, was expressed by Ashmore (1981:48) when she stated, "The problem is essentially that 'residence' comprises a complex set of activities, not all of which need necessarily be carried out at the same place, and 'dwellings' therefore constitute a polythetically defined set of forms, with no single list of universally necessary and sufficient material correlates." In light of this caveat, *house* in the present analysis is defined as that element of the built environment which minimally provides shelter to a set of occupants on a consistent basis. This definition follows that of McGuire and Schiffer (1983:280), who similarly identify the key role of the dwelling as the physical mediator between some consistent social unit and the external environment. This definition, with its anthropological roots stretching back to Malinowski (1960:83), intentionally eliminates other defining criteria such as social identity and psychic associations so as to simplify and make more direct the present analysis. It is certainly recognized that the conceptualization of "the house" or "the home" *exclusively* as mediator between its occupant(s) and the external environment is perhaps unrealized in the anthropological literature; it might exist only among some hunter-gatherer groups such as early Tasmanians (Bonwick 1967) and the Ona of Tierra del Fuego (Bennett 1963)—that is, groups that build only the most meager of self-protective features.

For the purposes of the present analysis, the architectural data from various Maya sites, and Copan in particular, suggest that there were minimally two basic forms of architectural design for residential structures: (1) the wattle and daub, or pole and thatch, structure and (2) the masonry, or dressed stone, structure. The former was associated principally with commoners, the latter with higher-status, elite households. Although I am cognizant of the fact that there was in reality a continuum of improvements (Haviland and Moholy-Magy 1992; Tourtellot, Sabloff, and Carmean 1992), this intentionally simplified dichotomy of residential forms best suits the heuristic needs of the present discussion and ensuing analyses.

In discussing architectural form, it is appropriate to incorporate the notion of a "template," or mental construct, of the idealized, expected form. When individuals decide to build a house, they do not start from scratch in terms of design, but rather base their decisions (either consciously or unconsciously) in part on the proven effectiveness of existing norms of design. This notion of an architectural template should not be equated with any statements concerning ultimate causality, but rather the more benign recognition that the discussion of stability and change in architectural form might benefit heuristically by incorporating the concept of an expected design template.

The Basic Architectural Form

The wattle and daub architectural form among the Maya is what I will call the *basic* form, synonymous with "folk," "popular," and "vernacular" architecture (Rapoport 1969:2). I prefer this term because it conveys both the source of energy (the household budget) and the level of energy (relatively low) expended on the house. There are certainly variations of the basic form within and among Maya sites, as there were and still are among Maya houses (Wauchope 1938). Nonetheless, there has been a remarkable conservatism in the basic form through time, and such houses, keeping size a constant, demanded very similar expenditures of energy in their construction.

The archetypal Maya basic house form (Figure 6) is typified by a low (10–30 cm) substructural platform of earth, stone, and debris, contained by a retaining wall of stone. The surface is tamped to serve as a floor for the residence and exterior porch. The rectilinear or curvilinear superstructure begins with a low (one or two courses) stone foundation wall upon which wattle and daub walls are erected, framed by from four to eight mainposts. These walls of daub—mud mixed with some aggregate such as sand, grass, or wood chips to prevent cracking—are susceptible to heavy wear through direct and indirect pounding of rainfall; as such, they are treated with a thin coat of lime-based wash. Finally, a roof of vegetal material—usually palm thatch or grass—is constructed. This roof is gabled; that is, the pitch (a

Figure 6. Example of the contemporary basic form in Copan
during the construction process.

mathematical expression of slope) falls in two directions from the ridgepole. The roof continues beyond the wooden frame, forming eaves on three sides and an overhang covering a front porch, which is an integral part of the residential structure. Very often the residence contains a kitchen, located against one side of the house. In these cases, the wall abutting the kitchen often does not reach the base of the roof, permitting smoke and heat to more readily exit the house. Perhaps the best-preserved illustrations of basic houses from a Maya site are from the Ceren site (Sheets 1992), where the dispersal of volcanic ash greatly inhibited the normal transformations affecting these houses.

The earliest known basic residence was discovered at the site of Cuello, Belize (Hammond and Gerhardt 1990; Hammond 1991a). Structure 329, dated to ca. 1100 B.C., is reconstructed as having been a wattle and daub superstructure built upon a low (10 cm) platform measuring approximately 12 × 8 m. This platform was constructed of earth supported by uncut cobble retaining walls and was apsidal (parallel walls with curved ends) in form. Currently, our most complete data concerning the evolution of architectural form come from Cuello.

Thus far, the earliest basic residence at Copan has been recovered from beneath the final courtyard surface of Courtyard A, Group 9N-8 (Fash 1983, 1991a:65). The structure, dated to the Early Preclassic period (1300–900 B.C.), is defined as residential based on its association with a wide range of domestic artifacts and organic materials. The platform is recorded as measuring 2.5 × 4 m, and, like Structure 329 at Cuello, was apsidal in form. The absence of post molds on the platform may be a consequence of transformations, particularly alluvial flooding, which destroyed differentially the perimeter of the residence.

As mentioned, there are numerous variations on the basic form. Local resource availability generally determines the materials in construction, such as thatch rather than grass as a roofing material. Local variations in architectural design also exist; for example, among the Chorti of Guatemala, a separate eave, rather than a simple extension of the roof, is built to protect the porch (Wisdom 1940:127). Nonetheless, these are essentially variations on a single theme; any comparative analysis of the material benefits and costs based on these variations would likely fail to identify any significant differences. Similarly, the differences in energetic investment in construction based solely on these variations are at best minor.

During all stages in the history and evolution of the Maya, the basic form dominated. During the peak of elite presence at Copan, this basic form represented minimally 85 percent of all residences (see Table 11 for calculations). The onset of this period in the evolution of the Copan polity witnessed a considerable increase in population, settlement, and architectural growth (Fash 1983; Webster and Freter 1990a, 1990b), and thus presumably periods before and after the Late Classic saw some higher percentage of basic house forms.

The Improved Architectural Form

Masonry residential architecture (Figure 7) has garnered such terms as "monumental" and "elite"; again, with the present energetic orientation in mind, I will term such architecture *improved*. This type of residential architecture has long been the center of archaeological research, and construction details are well established (Roys 1934; Pollock 1965). This architectural form exhibits greater variation than does the basic form since these residences are architecturally more complex (in terms of size of each building, number of

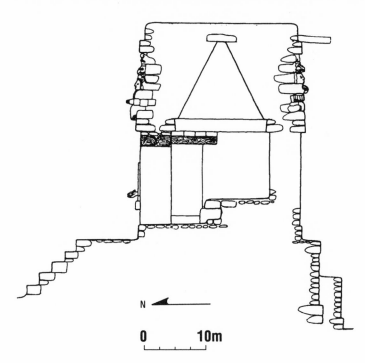

Figure 7. The improved form: *a*, Structure 9N-82C; *b*, cross-section of Structure 9N-82C
(modified from Fash 1989)

structural components, etc.), and they housed occupants holding positions of higher status within the hierarchy of social power; the buildings as media thus possessed greater political and symbolic value.

This improved form, following the terminology outlined by Loten and Pendergast (1984), was characterized by a variety of general features and components. The following architectural innovations were associated with the improved form: (1) lengthened and heightened substructural platform, with the addition of terraces at the expense of a porch; (2) dressed masonry blocks in the retaining wall of the substructure, supported by backing masonry and mortar; (3) increased proportion of stone to earth in the fill or hearting of the substructure; (4) a low building platform constructed upon the substructural surface, serving to outline the superstructure and provide a step onto the rooms of the superstructure; (5) a superstructure wall of double-faced masonry; (6) internal variations in room organization; (7) the presence of interior benches; (8) a beam and mortar roof or a vaulted roof containing a corbelled arch; (9) exterior sculptural decorations; and (10) a thick protective layer of plaster that covered the entire structure. Additional features could be cited, such as the presence of niches and cornices (Pollock 1965), and there is certainly room for debate concerning the statistical measurement of variation of the improved form.

As with the basic form, the improved form represents a single category with specific differences in architecture. For example, Roys (1934:91), Haviland (1985:110–115), and Loten and Pendergast (1984:8) all observe that masonry blocks can be distinguished on the basis of formal attributes, method of installment, and type or quality of mortar. On the basis of masonry alone, then, a large number of types and variations in residences could be created. Likewise, based on the elaboration of the substructure alone, Tourtellot (1988a) was able to create seven categories of dwellings at Seibal. Certainly, I endorse such classifications, which may be essential in analyses designed to chronologically seriate construction, reconstruct task units within the construction process, or generate better models of reuse of building materials. Similarly, greater categorization could be created based on the transitional stages or form of residences. As I suggest below, the improved form evolved from the basic form; thus logically as well as empirically there were numerous intermediary forms of residential design. Nonetheless, for the specific purposes of the present analyses, I am collapsing all residences with a masonry superstructure into the improved category.

A third hypothetical architectural form is associated with nomadic Archaic cultures in the southern lowlands. Research conducted on the central coast of Belize has identified the presence of Archaic hunter-gatherer groups dating to ca. 7000 B.C. (MacNeish, Wilkerson, and Nelken-Terner 1980). The only data relating to residential structures built by these early occupants of the Maya lowlands consist of a set of five post molds at Cuello that date to 2478–2305 B.C. (Hammond 1991a:26, 30). Notwithstanding, a huge gap exists in the archaeological record concerning residential architecture of the presedentary Maya. Although rockshelters and perhaps even the forest cover itself provided natural shelter for some or all of these populations, it is a reasonable hypothesis that these populations did in fact construct houses to meet the minimal criterion of providing shelter—the house as mediator between the human population and the external environment. There are a considerable number of covering laws concerning houses built by nomadic populations (Robbins 1966; Whiting and Ayres 1968; McGuire and Schiffer 1983) from which this hypothetical house form can be constructed. First, the low population of these initial microbands would suggest a small size for the structure, with perhaps only one or two structures simultaneously occupied in any single camp. Second, the band's episodic and short-term sedentism would suggest limited expected use-life of the house (McGuire and Schiffer 1983) and thus very low energetic investment in labor and materials. As such, only local materials that were easy to procure and assemble would be considered, and these structures would likely be built directly on the prepared ground surface rather than on a substructure (cf. Pyburn 1990; Wilk and Wilhite 1991). Third, the impermanence and limited use of the house would suggest a curvilinear form, a design that minimizes construction effort at the expense of interior space. Interestingly, this hypothesized curvilinear design for the residence of nomadic populations may have served as a template for houses built by those early sedentary populations at both Cuello and perhaps Copan.

Given favorable depositional contexts, it is almost certain that sufficient data will eventually be recovered to test this hypothesis. Perhaps early settlements along terraces adjacent to very small rivers or streams (thus possibly having avoided later large-scale destruction) would offer the greatest potential for recovery of such data. On a less optimistic note, ethnographic data from nomadic hunter-gatherer groups such as the Siriono (Holmberg 1969) indicate that structures may have been built and occupied for extended periods of time without leaving any archaeological remains. The Siriono build expanded lean-tos by lashing two connected poles between the trunks of two standing trees, against which palm thatch is placed. No posts are dug and no manufactured materials such as daub are used. Regardless, the Cuello data are very encouraging, and future research will likely recover the antecedents of the wattle and daub platformed structures built by the sedentary Maya.

The Emergence of the Improved Form

It has long been recognized that the improved form evolved from the basic form in design and, in part, construction (Thompson 1892; Wauchope 1938:150). Certainly the patterns of change in the design and form of housing were multilinear and site-specific, with variable rates of change witnessed among Maya centers. We currently possess some data which serve as a first approximation for the general timing of the transition from the basic to the improved form.

At Copan the initial notable improvement in architecture is evident during the late Bijac phase (A.D. 100–400). Ca. A.D. 350 several structures were built in the Great Plaza that, although currently unquantified, indicate cost improvements beyond the basic form. Structure 10L-sub-2 is a large masonry walled platform measuring 85 m × 18 m that presumably housed some members of the emergent elite, quite possibly in a large wattle and daub superstructure (Cheek 1983). Similarly, Structures 10L-26-6 and 10L-sub-6-3 were built at this time, the former bearing masonry retaining walls on its preserved platform. This set of three structures, all of which may have been residential, formed a courtyard group collectively with platforms of higher-quality stonework and greater horizontal dimensions, which at Copan represent the initial type of improvement in residential form.

At about this same time, one structure in Group 9N-8 is built with a cobble platform of significantly greater size, measuring 50 m × 12 m (Fash 1991a:73). In addition, it is at this time that architectural revision is evident in the East Court (Sharer, Miller, and Traxler 1992). Although all of these changes require energetic quantification if we are to more fully assess their meaning in sociopolitical terms, it appears that the initial architectural manifestations of power differentials appeared at Copan during the Early Classic period.

These architectural improvements appear somewhat earlier at many other Maya sites of the southern lowlands perhaps reflecting Copan's specific and later evolutionary trajectory of sociopolitical complexity. The first use of cut-stone masonry and lime plaster at Tikal was associated with Structure 5D-sub-14-3, dating to the Late Preclassic Chuen phase (250 B.C. – 100 B.C.; Culbert 1977:38). The earliest evidence for a corbelled arch at Tikal comes from Structure 5C-54 and is dated to the Cauac phase (100 B.C. –A.D. 150). Adams (1977:82) reported that at Becan there is an increase in the use of stone in

construction at the onset of the Pakluum phase (50 B.C.–A.D. 250). Willey
(1977:147) noted that the corbelled arch makes its first appearance at Altar
de Sacrificios in the period A.D. 1–300. Sites such as El Mirador, which
reached their apex of sociopolitical and architectural complexity in the Late
Preclassic period, presumably began improving beyond the basic form during the Middle Preclassic period (Matheny 1980). The most detailed evidence
for the gradual addition of improvements in architecture comes from Cuello
(Hammond and Gerhardt 1990; Hammond 1991a). At that site, residential
platforms undergo changes in size (both lateral and vertical) and stone quality
beginning ca. 800 B.C., and the earliest identifiable pyramid (Structure 351)
is built ca. A.D. 75 (Hammond and Gerhardt 1990:472). Although each site
must be considered on an individual basis, it appears that the initial changes
in the basic form, beginning with improvements in the substructural platform and ending with the use of masonry for superstructural walls, began
during the Middle or Late Preclassic period at most large Maya sites.

These improvements are first evidenced in the general ethnological context of ranked societies (Fried 1967). Hypothetically, at this juncture in the
evolution of societal complexity, architectural change should be characterized by a significant increase in the quality of a few residences, the majority
remaining unchanged. Incremental expansion in the scale of ranking should
then increase the quality of those emergent "elite" structures and simultaneously increase to some degree the overall quality of the basic residence
(Abrams 1989). Only with the quantification of a large sample of architecture
from ranked systems instituted by the southern lowland Maya, however, will
this hypothesis be subject to more complete testing.

The Determinants of Form

The consideration of the "determinants," or primary influences, of architectural form has had a surprisingly long history within anthropology, in part
since it served as a vehicle in broader paradigmatic struggles. Amos Rapoport, in his classic *House Form and Culture* (1969:47), perhaps crystallized the
modern theoretical debate over form when he stated that "what finally de-
cides the form of a dwelling . . . is the vision that people have of the ideal
life." This perspective—that one's mental template ultimately determines
form—has been embraced by a large number of scholars. Hillier and Hanson
(1984:5), to cite but one example, caution against the reduction of any explanation of space "to being only a by-product of external causative agents."

Various dimensions of this perspective have been countered by advocates
of cultural materialism and a processual approach in archaeology (Harris

1979; Price 1982; Binford 1989). Some of the fundamental responses focus on the methodological inaccessibility of "internal causative agents" and the lack of definition and recognition of those factors which produce one's "visions." I suspect that one's vision of the ideal is greatly influenced by those external realities within one's sight. In addition, a materialist or selectionist perspective is justified on the grounds that houses are certainly, if not foremost, technomic artifacts that tend to conform to cost-benefit analysis. Moreover, adopting the perspective that decisions are ultimately based on unique cultural properties, placing priority on "culture" as a purely mentalistic construct, has perhaps led archaeology into what has been termed the "terminal skeptical crisis" (Watson 1986:450), the logic of which effectively makes archaeological reconstruction impossible and the evaluation of archaeological reconstruction entirely a matter of politics and sociometry.

The approach taken in the present work is predicated on the recognition that individuals tend to assign value to components of their world, whether they be raw materials, authority, affection, or the like, and that similar cultural contexts produce probabilistically similar valuations, and thus behavioral decisions (Steward 1955). Acceptance of this principle makes possible an interpretation of the past through analogous reasoning measured against the empirical archaeological data. This position was made quite clear by Watson, LeBlanc, and Redman (1984:259), who stated that "the basic principle of all archaeological interpretation is analogical." If models and analogs are accepted as viable means of interpreting the unobservable past, then those models most appropriate, following a materialist perspective, are systemic, diachronic, and, very importantly, hierarchic (Price 1982). Finally, any model must be subjected to the rigors of science, which serves as a charter (in the Malinowskian sense), guiding the conduct of evaluation of models against the empirical archaeological data.

My reliance on a more materialistic, analytic approach is not a statement of denial of nonmaterial variables. These perspectives are far from monolithic; certainly no paradigm can claim a monopoly over the diverse variables that produce the complexities of human culture. In fact, analytically these positions can be combined within the overarching model of cultural selection, the central analytic components being variation, transmission, and cultural selection (Campbell 1965; Harris 1979; Price 1982; Rindos 1984; Sanderson 1990). Within this model, the origins of architectural form become moot, variation being present in all societies. However, individuals are not omniscient, and variation is clearly influenced by mental templates, accounting in part for the conservativeness of the evolutionary process. Similarly, behaviors can be selected for or against, in part on the basis of conceptions of the expected life. Consistent with a materialist perspective, they tend, however, to be overwhelmingly selected for or against on the basis of their impact on the individual's biopsychological quality of life. Nonetheless, the hierarchic modeling of variables within the selectionist paradigm allows for the inclusion of mentalistic as well as materialistic variables.

In sum, this very brief theoretical discourse reveals my clear bias for a cultural selectionist model in reconstructing the archaeological past. Furthermore, this discourse has helped direct discussion by suggesting that the importance of analyzing residential form lies less in considering the origins of form than in studying the material consequences of living within various forms of architecture.

Material Consequences of the Basic and Improved Forms

Now it is necessary to consider the comparative effects on the occupants of both elemental architectural forms at Copan, the biopsychological consequences forming the dominant basis for the selection process. The improved residential form, characterized by various traits, the most important being the presence of a masonry superstructure, provided a range of material and behavioral benefits beyond those offered by the wattle and daub superstructure with a thatched roof. Following the materialist orientation presented above, I argue that these biopsychological distinctions underlie the more symbolic associations with the two forms of housing and, from an energetic and evolutionary perspective, provided the context for generating the high ideological value assigned to masonry architecture.

This hypothesis—that masonry structures represented a high material as well as symbolic value relative to the basic residential form—has not always been accepted, principally owing to the "adaptive" quality of the wattle and daub residence. Totten (1926:29), for example, stated, "The adobe [wattle and daub] of the Indian today, though simple and inexpensive to construct, is a perfect example of adaptation to conditions of a tropical climate." Fitch and Branch (1960), in a general ecological overview of house form, correctly noted that thatched roofs in the humid tropics expand when wet, thus effectively shedding water, and contract when dry, thus providing for better interior ventilation. These statements tend to obfuscate the fact that various socioeconomic, political, and ideological conditions involving *limited* resource access strongly influence the decision to build this type of housing. While they may be "adaptations" (i.e., expressed responses to needs), they do not necessarily represent the best of all possible forms. Interestingly, the concept that wattle and daub structures are somehow more "fit" may be in part a consequence of the conspicuous archaeological nature of the contrasting stone structures, again following the leitmotiv that the archaeological remains themselves influence the perceptions of archaeologists, particularly concerning architecture. In considering the notion that masonry structures are somehow less "fit" for the humid tropics, we should remember that masonry structures were built and occupied by the prehistoric Maya for over 1,000 years—hardly a "maladaptation" in the general sense—and that far greater numbers of wattle and daub structures physically failed in their primary role as mediators between their occupants and the external environment. Finally, in the ensuing discussion of relative benefits, the costs of construction and maintenance are not considered; ironically, one could argue that the costs of construction and maintenance of masonry structures were far less than those of wattle and daub structure to the *occupants* of these structures since the elite themselves almost surely did not physically participate in the actual construction process.

Fire Resistance. Perishable structures, constructed principally of wood and vegetal roofing material, are of course much more susceptible to fire than masonry structures. This is especially true when the house also serves as a kitchen. Studies conducted on tuff, the igneous stone that was ubiquitously used as the medium for masonry architecture at Copan, have highlighted the fact that this specific stone is highly fire-resistant (Zalessky 1966), adding in part to this clear material distinction. Interestingly, I was told by the head of one household in Copan that he preferred thatch to grass, despite having to import it, due to its greater resistance to fire. So it is not surprising that the first major improvement in the house by contemporary Copanecos is to replace the grass roof with corrugated steel, or *lámina*. This desire to replace the organic roof with some inorganic material such as metal or tiles is paralleled throughout Honduras. Based on a survey of rural housing conducted in 1965, it was estimated that 78.7 percent of rural houses still had earthen floors, whereas only 25.6 percent of those houses had organic (grass or straw) roofs (Koth, Silva, and Dietz 1965:243). Thus replacement of the organic roof is clearly the first priority in improving the quality of the contemporary basic house.

Thermal Regulation. As stated earlier, the critical function of houses is to serve as an effective mediator between the human occupants and the external environment. One primary aspect of this mediation is the minimizing of internal variations in temperature. It has repeatedly been confirmed that stone as a building material better regulates the internal temperature than does mud, adobe, or wood. The thermophysical properties of stone allow heat from outside to be better absorbed, thus minimizing the transfer of that heat to the interior of the house (Givoni 1969:113). In addition, the greater heat capacity of stone as a wall and roof material serves to release heat at a slower rate, providing more heat for the interior of the house during the cooler nights. Finally, the thickness of stone masonry walls also enhances the thermal regulation qualities of stone as a building material—thus the best temperature control is provided by those structures with the thickest masonry walls bearing vaulted roofs.

Heating Costs. The size of individual rooms varies considerably between the basic form and the improved form. Rooms in the improved form tend to be smaller, self-contained, and more enclosed units, whereas those in the basic form are in effect one large room partitioned into spaces that are physically connected. This difference in room size has an influence on the ability to heat individual rooms, particularly during the cooler nights. During the winter evenings at Copan, the temperature can drop as low as 30 degrees F. The smaller, self-contained rooms of the improved form would have been better heat retainers; in addition, they would have been easier and more efficient to heat in terms of fuelwood needs. The more open spaces within the basic form would have led to greater heat loss and a less efficient use of fuelwood. Notably, then, the elite, who had better access to fuelwood, required less of this important raw material to heat their homes.

Increased Platform Height. Masonry substructures are typically greater in their vertical dimension than those associated with the basic form. As such, these structures may be better protected from flooding and rainy conditions in general. In addition, they provided more breeze, which may have created more comfortable surroundings for the occupants.

Health Conditions: Resistance to Insects. This last distinction between forms may have had the greatest impact on the occupants of these residences (here I will discuss only those aspects of health that can be directly linked to housing). As microenvironments, these two house forms constitute very different media for the harboring and transmitting of diseases and thus may have had a direct impact on the physical and psychological well-being of the occupants. First, the roofing materials are notably different. Dwellings with grass or thatched roofs are notorious as loci for disease-bearing protozoa (Acha and Szyfres 1980:380). Shimkin (1973) was perhaps the first to accentuate this particular aspect of health and housing by focusing attention on Chagas' disease, or American trypsanosomiasis. This protozoan disease is transmitted to the human host by assassin bugs (*Triatoma infestans* and others); as Shimkin (1973:279) stated, "Assassin bugs are very difficult to exterminate in native houses with extensive thatching, cracks, and other hiding places. Abandonment or even burning of the structure may be essential." This association has been noted by other scholars: for example, Way (1981:277–278) confirms that "American trypsanosomiasis is often maintained as a human infection when thatched roofing provides a shelter for the vector near humans" (also Whitlaw and Chaniotis 1978; Coimbra 1988:85).

A second major health distinction involves the flooring material—a plastered versus a tamped dirt surface. The World Health Organization, emphasizing that the domestic environment is the front line against diseases, observed that "dirt floors not only make domestic hygiene difficult, but may harbor helminths" (1989:8). Helminths include such parasites as hookworms and ringworms, and anyone who has seen individuals infected with these organisms will immediately recognize the importance of prevention. These types of diseases would logically most infect those individuals spending the majority of their time in and around the house, namely women and children. Dirt floors further decrease the hygienic quality of the basic house by providing a safe niche for the assassin bugs responsible for Chagas' disease. Since the heating requirements were greater for basic houses, fuelwood was likely stored in or around the house. In their study of Chagas' disease in Costa Rica, Zeledon et al. (1975:222) concluded that "dirt floors and the use of firewood should be considered among the principal socioeconomic and cultural factors used to define the epidemiologic profile of Chagas' disease in Costa Rica." They note that the assassin bugs live both in the thatching of roofs and in the fuelwood brought into the house, and that they instinctively bore into the dirt floors for added protection.

This epidemiological aspect of dirt floors then enhances the value of plaster as a component of residential forms. The courtyards, for example, associated with the improved house form were at least partially surfaced with thick plaster, and evidence of resurfacing is quite common. Based on detailed analysis of artifacts and their spatial distributions and associations at Copan (Hendon 1991), it is clear that portions of the courtyard surface itself were used as activity areas involving food preparation. Presumably, a plaster rather than an earthen surface in a domestic environment associated with food preparation would increase to some degree hygienic quality. Certainly the ability to keep the plaster surface cleaner in terms of waste removal would be enhanced. The fact that children, for example, play on these surfaces would make the cleaner plaster courtyard a better and safer environment than tamped earthen surfaces.

A final hygienic distinction between a plaster and earth courtyard surface is linked to the more efficient removal of water provided by the plaster surface. Water drainage can be more readily controlled on a surface that has been leveled, prepared with a subsurface grouting, and plastered. Earthen surfaces surrounding houses tend to provide less efficient drainage of water, thus providing niches for the accumulation of standing pools of water, which may then harbor insects detrimental to the quality of the residents' health. In addition, improved structures often had drainage features along both their front and back.

Although it could be argued that all of the above distinctions between the two house forms are hypothetical, requiring empirical data for confirmation, in many cases we are considering homologous rather than analogous entities. Grass does burn more readily than stone; it does today, and it did in the past. Similarly, insects do infest organic roofs rather than plastered masonry roofs, and these insects still serve as hosts to protozoa that infect humans. Essentially, the distinctions between forms are based on physical properties rather than cultural values. Of course, the improved residence was not superior in all aspects to the basic dwelling. For example, masonry walls are characterized by relatively low elasticity, making them more susceptible to structural failure (from incremental stress or sudden shocks from, say, earthquakes). However, in general, the comparison of these two forms strongly suggests that the masonry residences provided a significantly higher biopsychological quality of life to their occupants. Given the number of benefits provided by masonry structures, I have little doubt that Maya parents living at Copan at A.D. 700 had any problem recognizing the importance of the material distinctions between these house forms.

Large masonry structures have been viewed by some as having had negative effects on the Late Classic Maya, implicated as a drain of natural resources, the cause of overtaxation and subsequent revolt and ultimate collapse, and a symbol of the excesses of the elite. As a recurrent theme throughout this book, I would argue that the physical remains of large-scale architecture, as part of our first-level observations and interpretations (Binford 1989), far exaggerate the negative impact these structures had on the Maya. Regardless of one's subjective assessment of these structures, this comparison of house types can be furthered through a more quantified approach, the subject of the ensuing chapter and the methodological core of the following analyses.

4

The Energetics
of Construction

Within the context of general scientific inquiry, energetics involves the measurement of energy (in some form) and its transformations within a defined system (Odum 1971). As a method of analysis, it is well established in such disciplines as biochemistry, ecology, physics, and geology. In the context of cultural systematics, energetics involves the quantification of the processes of harnessing, moving, and consuming energy within a cultural system. Since most archaeologists feel epistemologically committed to the analysis of empirical remains of past cultures, energetics in this context is defined as the method of quantifying the energy expended in those activities associated with the production, distribution, and consumption of materials within a cultural system. The evolutionary principle underlying an energetic approach is that people tend to adopt more energy-efficient behaviors and institutions over less efficient alternatives, with energetics providing the methodology through which this can be scientifically modeled and tested. Arguments against energetic analyses in archaeology are almost exclusively directed at its specific application rather than the logic and principle underlying energetics per se (e.g., Webster 1981).

Energetics as a Method

When used by social scientists, energetics involves the translation of behavior into some form of energy as a common currency for analysis. This currency need not be energy in the elemental form of heat; energy in the form of labor-time or money may be acceptable equivalents to heat energy (Odum 1971). Thus an architectural energetic analysis that translates construction behaviors into labor costs is completely consistent with an energetic perspective.

One of the important aspects of the present energetic approach is the movement beyond volumetric studies, which may simply equate volume with cost. Equating volume with cost ignores the variations in labor costs. For example, two structures of equal size but in very different locations may require very different costs in terms of the transport of raw materials to the construction site. These differentials are obscured through simple volumetrics.

Energetics necessitates a systemic perspective in its application, but it should not be equated with theory, just as "systems theory" is more a method of modeling relationships than an endorsement of any theoretical stance (Watson, LeBlanc, and Redman 1984). Nonetheless, energetics is more congruent with a materialist or ecological framework since the energetic method necessarily targets only those quantifiable material components of a cultural system.

The essential advantage of an energetic approach in the reconstruction of past cultural institutions is that it analytically eliminates intersubjective assessments of material culture, an approach necessary for scientific inquiry (Harris 1968). Ever since the publication of *Houses and House-life of the American Aborigines* by Lewis Henry Morgan in 1881, anthropologists have accepted the rather obvious observation that greater size and quality of architecture correlate in some general sense with increased cultural complexity, however the latter is defined. The critical value of an energetic approach is that it provides a means of explicitly defining subjective assessments of scale and quality, or in the present context, cost, thus making possible an array of analyses otherwise unavailable. This critical need for comparative, quantitative analysis, provided through energetics, becomes conspicuous when absent. For example, the scale of architectural construction at the Maya site of Caracol, Belize, has recently been described as "massive," an obvious conclusion given a population estimate of perhaps 400,000 (Chase, Chase, and Haviland 1990:502). However, the scale of architectural construction at Classic Copan has similarly been described as "massive" (Fash 1983:247, 254); yet the maximal population estimate for Copan is only about 25,000 (Webster and Freter 1990b:82). In effect, conclusions concerning the Maya are still being based on the observation that the buildings are in fact large. Clearly, if we are to participate in any scientific study of architecture in archaeology, then we have an obligation to investigate methods that transcend simplistic and subjective assessments.

Various energetic methods tend to differ in their degree of specificity and application. Erasmus' (1965) work at Uxmal involved the rather detailed quantification of construction labor costs derived through replication of tasks applied to measurable volumes of civic architecture. A far wider range of structures has been similarly quantified from Tikal, albeit most of these structures remain unexcavated. As a consequence, a very general collective cost per structure was offered (Arnold and Ford 1980). At Sayil, excavated structures representing an intermediate range of social statuses were quantified on the basis of the comparative volume of faced masonry walls translated into person-days (Carmean 1991; Tourtellot, Sabloff, and Carmean 1992). Quantitative analysis of architecture at Copan was initiated by Cheek (1986), who quantified a sample of Classic structures on the basis of relative basal platform volumes. To date, Cheek's analysis is the only diachronic quantified study of Maya architecture. Although these analyses differ in various ways, each is consistent in that the degree of specificity in the method of quantification best fit the quality of architectural detail. Thus, these are not competing methods but rather different methods given different architectural data.

In my own research at Copan, the energetic application was relatively specific owing to the very large and detailed architectural database produced as a consequence of the PAC II research design. Thus, the method here is somewhat different from those used in the analyses cited above. As stated earlier, the goal is to reduce by some order of magnitude the subjective assessments of architectural scale or cost for use in comparative analyses. The method below satisfies this goal but should in no way be taken as the only method of quantification.

The quantification of energy from architecture requires the combining of rates of work per task with the volume of raw materials per structure. As stated earlier, the specificity with which one can apply this method is a function of the level of architectural detail available to the researcher; fortunately, the PAC II excavations at Copan were designed to expose a large number of structures in their complete final form as well as to extensively trench those structures to expose earlier construction episodes. This rather detailed archaeological method thus provides the researcher with the means to assess volumetrics of materials per structure and, in concert with estimates of cost per task in the construction process, distance to raw materials, and weight of the raw material, to generate a total labor cost per structure. Counterbalancing this detail for Late Classic structures is the relative scarcity of comparable data for earlier periods. Thus the quantification, while broad-based and relatively detailed, is synchronic.

The costs generated in this analysis are approximations of some ultimately unknowable "truth" or reality. The costs of construction are recognized as estimates *most directly* since we lack control over all of the variables that affected the actual construction process. For example, the varying densities of the soil and the conditions under which that specific soil was dug affect the rate of procurement (ECAFE 1957:16, Table 7). On a more extreme level, the comparative energetic efficiencies of varying biomechanical options, or ergonomics, cannot be presumed to be known in a complete sense (e.g., Zhu and Zhang 1990); thus, even simple acts such as walking or carrying can yield distinct energetic values. In the following discussion I will be as explicit as possible in highlighting those tasks over which we have less control.

Approximations are generated, furthermore, owing to the fact that not all costs associated with construction were expended in the actual creation of the building. For example, glyphic data indicate that various dedicatory and mortuary rituals accompanied the construction process (e.g., Freidel and Schele 1989; Schele and Miller 1986). These rituals certainly occurred in association with architecture in the Main Group at Copan. Current data also strongly suggest that dedicatory rituals accompanied construction of some masonry structures in the surrounding urban barrio. As a case in point, Feature 29 is a vessel placed beneath the plastered floor surface in Room 8, Structure 9N-82 (Webster, Fash, and Abrams 1986:179, 297). Since the plaster floor over the vessel was not disturbed (i.e., resurfaced), we know that the vessel was placed there during the original floor construction, and glyphic data (Schele 1989:74) support the interpretation that vessels placed beneath floors served in some dedicatory capacity. In addition, basic rural structures have also been associated with dedicatory artifacts, such as the complete Copador vessel recovered from the fill of Structure 7D-2-2 (Gonlin 1993). By analogy, Wauchope (1938:143) noted that, upon the completion of a Maya commoner house, a hole was dug in the center of the floor in which was placed holy water, a chicken, and silver. Thus it is probable that dedicatory rituals consumed energy and thus added to the cost of construction of residences on all social levels at Copan. Despite the energy expended in rituals, however, the costs in materials and time generated from the conduct of these rituals are not incorporated into the cost of construction.

In addition, no allowance has been made in the estimation of costs for the fluctuating value of labor. Although this question of labor value may seem anachronistic given the lack of a market principle affecting the supply and demand (and thus market value) of labor at prehispanic Maya centers, the value of labor does fluctuate in nonmarket economies. Currently, however, we have no direct means of discerning the fluctuations in labor value. Arguably, population dynamics (reflecting the size of the labor force) relative to demand for that labor should provide a comparative measure or baseline for changes in labor value. I would suggest, however, that such an analysis be directed at agricultural labor rather than construction labor, since the former will provide a more secure context for generating marginal productivity reflective of labor value.

Finally, the house itself can be conceived of as embodying several values: a use value and exchange value, following Marx, as well as what could be considered a social or moral value, following Mauss. In the present analysis, the energetic costs are approximations of use value, the direct energy expended in production. It is presumed at this stage of analysis that houses were not produced explicitly for exchange and thus were not commodities per se, subject to exchange values.

Construction Costs

Since direct evidence of actual construction costs at Late Classic Copan is of course lacking, the present analysis is based on ethnographic data varying in substance and degree of reliability. Contemporary construction in the region involves many of the same raw materials as those used in the Classic period. This fact permits control for idiosyncracies of local geography and distribution of raw materials—a set of parameters that may account for discrepancies between this and others conducted elsewhere (e.g., Erasmus 1965).

Data collection was conducted during restoration activities undertaken as part of PAC II. During this restoration, actual timed observations of effectively normal rhythms of work were recorded (Abrams 1984a). These observations provided a more reliable basis for quantifying energetic costs than data collected through questionnaires or recall. "Natural" observations were supplemented with "experimental" data, especially designed to address questions of the labor costs resulting from technological differences (e.g., stone versus steel tools) and to estimate costs of tasks such as sculpturing, performed only rarely if at all in the present, normal course of building.

In addition, I conducted a preliminary survey of households in 1981 in order to better understand contemporary Copaneco houses and house construction. The data consisted of the size of the house, the materials used in construction, the seasonality of construction, and the personnel involved in the building process. These data, as they apply to wattle and daub structures, are presented in Table 2. A fuller set of data on peasant houses at Copan has

Table 2. Household Survey Data, Copan, 1981

House[a]	Area (m^2)	Labor Source	Days	P-D[b]	Season	Roof Type
2	39	Owner (male), two friends	16	48	Feb.	Lámina
3	44	Owner (male), son, friend	48	144	Jul–Aug.	Lámina
5	33	Owner (male)	42	42	Apr.?	Tile
6	28	Owner (male), two friends	18	54	Jan.–Apr.	Lámina
7	46	Owner (male), two neighbors	26	78	Feb.	Lámina
8	25	Owner (male), three friends	40	160	May	Lámina
9	64	Owner (male), three friends	34	136	?	Tile
10	48	Owner (male), wife, sister-in-law	28	84	Feb.	Tile
12	23	Owner (male)	24	24	?	Grass
13	49	Owner (male), son	33	66	?	½ lámina, ½ palm
16	33	Owner (male)	33	33	Oct.	Palm
17	37	Owner (male), brother	30	60	?	Lámina
19	45	Owner (male), brother, neighbor	11	33	?	Lámina
20	23	Owner (male)	30	30	?	Grass
23	23	Owner (male)	28	28	Feb.–Apr.	Grass

Source: Abrams 1984
[a]Original house number assigned in survey.
[b]Person-Days

been compiled (Abrams 1984a:275–287, Appendix D); here I have excluded from this broader sample those structures which were not the basic wattle and daub house form.

Some general characteristics concerning the building process are evident from these data. First, construction in Copan is generally undertaken during the dry season, from January to May. The reasons are rather predictable: dry conditions provide for dry materials and better working conditions, and the agricultural off-season provides the necessary time for scheduling house construction. Houses are generally built within a one-month period, a consequence of their functional import. In addition, house construction is a male activity, although on occasion women assist in the project. When considering residential construction among the prehispanic Copanecos, I tend to attribute these characteristics to the earlier culture based on the continuities between ancient and modern Maya houses as well as the physical parameters that remain consistent through time.

Overall building costs were first divided into the following major formation processes, or operations: (1) procurement of raw materials, (2) transport, (3) manufacture, and (4) actual construction or assembly. In addition, lateral recycling and reuse were considered in the total formation process. However, the data regarding earlier substructural construction episodes are less detailed than those for final episodes of construction, making the quantification of previous razed structures difficult. The question of reuse is discussed in more detail below.

Units of time were measured in person-hours (p-h) or person-days (p-d), standard units of labor-time. For this analysis, a five-hour workday was considered appropriate for performing strenuous tasks such as quarrying tuff, excavating earth, and transporting materials (cf. Erasmus 1965), while an eight-hour workday was deemed appropriate for performing less strenuous tasks such as carving masonry blocks, sculpturing, and actual construction. The present methodology does not adjust for the fact that tasks differ in difficulty and physiological costs, which is perhaps irrelevant since specific divisions of labor (by age and gender) are unknown. Table 3 summarizes the average costs for each of the component tasks in construction. An amplification of these costs is necessary since (1) methods must be made explicit if they are to be of use in comparative analyses and (2) the present method differs from that described in the original quantification of Copan architecture (Abrams 1984a, 1987, 1989). It should be noted that refinements to the original method have simplified the application of the method without altering in any significant way the conclusions drawn in those earlier applications;

Table 3. Operations, Tasks, and Costs per Task in Construction

Procurement
   Earth: 2.6 m³/p-d
   Cobbles: 7,200 kg/p-d
   Tuff: 750 kg/p-d

Transport

$$\text{m}^3/\text{p-d} = Q \times \frac{1}{(^L/_v + ^L/_{v'})} \times H$$

Manufacture
   Dressed masonry: 1 m³/11.6 p-d
   Rough cobbles: 1 m³/1.16 p-d
   Plaster: 1 m³/43.9 p-d
   Sculpture: simple $= 321$ cm²/p-h
            complex $= 89$ cm²/p-h

Construction
   Fine fill and superstructural wall fill: 4.8 m³/p-d
   All walls: 0.8 m³/p-d
   Cobble subflooring: 9.6 m²/p-d
   Plastering: 80 m²/p-d
   Wattle and daub superstructure: P-D $= -13.838 + 1.832$ (area)
   Champa: P-D $= \dfrac{-13.838 + 1.832 \text{ (area)}}{10}$

in fact, refinements are to be expected if we view science as the dynamic construction of approximations. These refinements will be summarized after the costs used in the method have been described. Table 4 provides an example of the application of these data in generating the cost estimate for Structure 9M-195B (see Figure 13), which the reader may wish to consult during the following presentation of energetic data.

Energetic Data

The data on quarrying were obtained by observing a worker quarrying in designed replicative experiments and by interviewing the supervisor of a local quarrying operation associated with the restoration process. In the replicative experiment, one man, somewhat experienced in quarrying, was hired

Table 4. Quantification of Structure 9M-195B

Procurement
Tuff: 101 m³ measured on structure
101/0.55 = 183.6 m³ quarried × 1,836 = 337,156 kg/750 = 450 p-d
Earth: 136 m³ measured in structure
136/2.6 = 52 p-d
Cobbles: 90 m³ measured in structure
90 × 1,863 = 225,810 kg/7,200 = 23 p-d

Transport
Tuff: 183.6/0.1 = 1,836 p-d
Earth: 136/1.89 = 72 p-d
Cobbles: 90/0.27 = 333 p-d
Plaster: 14.02/0.05 = 280 p-d

Manufacture
Masonry: 101 × 11.6 = 1,172 p-d
Sculpture: (complex motifs): 2.1 m² measured on structure =
21,000 cm² @ 89 cm²/p-h = 235.9 hrs/8 = 29 p-d
Plaster: 14.02 × 43.9 = 616 p-d

Construction
Masonry walls: 101/0.8 = 126 p-d
Fine fill: 123/4.8 = 26 p-d
Cobble surface: 72/9.6 = 8 p-d
Plaster surface: 350 m²/10 = 35 p-d
TOTAL = 5,058 p-d

to excavate tuff from a local outcrop (Figure 8). Using steel tools, this man could procure 715.6 kg of tuff in 2 hours and 23 minutes, or roughly 300 kg/p-h. This figure converts to 200 kg/p-h for stone tools, using a ratio of steel to stone of 1:1.5 (see below). Assuming a five-hour workday, the quarrying cost derived from this experiment was 1,000 kg/p-d.

The second source of quarrying data—interviews with a local quarry supervisor—yielded a somewhat different figure. These data yielded a quarrying cost of 153 kg/p-h, which converts to 102 kg/p-h using stone tools, or about 500 kg/p-d. Given these figures of 500 and 1,000 kg/p-d, the average, 750 kg/p-d, was used as the standard quarrying cost.

The volume of quarried stone can be derived only from the known

Figure 8. Quarrying tuff

volume of masonry as measured on the structure. Based on the ratio of the volume of the quarried stone to the volume of the finished masonry block, it was determined that a significant amount of waste was produced in the form of tuff chips and small fragments, even with the workers using steel tools; in fact, approximately half of the quarried block was lost in the manufacturing of dressed masonry. Specifically, to derive the volume of quarried stone, the masonry volume was divided by 0.55. This volume, in m^3, must then be converted into weight. I repeated several weighings of stone and, in conjunction with known volumes, estimated that the standard weight of tuff was 1,836 kg /m^3. Thus the volume of quarried tuff multiplied by 1,836 kg and divided by 750 kg yielded the cost of quarrying tuff.

The standard cost of procuring cobbles was obtained through timed observations of men collecting cobbles from a natural accumulation, or point bar, along the Copan River. One person, working eight hours, could procure 7,200 kg of cobbles. As with the standard weight of tuff, I weighed several generic cobbles and estimated that, on average, their weight was 1,863 kg /m^3. Thus I arrived at the cost of procurement of cobbles by taking the volume of cobbles from architectural measurements, multiplying by 1,863 kg, and then dividing by 7,200 kg.

In lieu of conducting earth-digging experiments, I have relied upon Erasmus' research (1965:285), which concluded that, in a five-hour day, one man could excavate 2.6 m³ of earth using wooden tools.

To derive the amount of cobbles and earth from the volume of fill, I took several profiles from trenches excavated into various buildings and estimated the ratio of earth to stone. Not surprisingly, the larger improved structures—those with extensive masonry superstructures—contained the largest volume of stone in their platform fill. Structure 9N-82C, for example, contained 47 percent cobbles and 53 percent earth while Structure 9N-80 contained 24 percent cobbles, and 76 percent earth. In general, the ratio of cobbles to earth was 1:2.

In lieu of conducting experiments involving the transport of various weights of raw materials, a standard formula, derived from UN experiments concerning manual versus mechanical transport, was used (ECAFE 1957: 22). Unfortunately, several metamorphoses of the original formula have been offered, and thus a presentation of all formulae is necessary. The original UN formula for manual transport of earth is as follows:

$$\text{Output} = Q \times \frac{60}{(^L/_v + ^L/_{v'} + c + d + e)} \times H,$$

where Q = quantity of earth per load, L = lead, or transport distance (m), V = velocity (loaded), V' = velocity (unloaded), c = loading time, d = unloading time, e = idle time, and H = hours per day; output is expressed in m³.

This formula was then simplified by Aaberg and Bonsignore (1975:46):

$$\text{Output} = Q \times \frac{1}{(^L/_v + ^L/_{v'})} \times H.$$

This formula eliminates loading and unloading time, converts minutes (60) into hours (1), and assumes $V = 3$ (km traveled with load) and $V' = 5$ (km traveled unloaded).

This formula was then *erroneously* copied in Abrams (1984a) as the following:

$$\text{Output} = Q \times \frac{1}{^L/_v} + \frac{1}{^L/_{v'}} \times H.$$

This formula greatly *increases* the capacity to move raw materials, thus decreasing time and labor, which is interesting given the fact that, based on this incorrect formula, the transport costs were the highest of all costs calculated at the time.

The Aaberg and Bonsignore formula was then again used in architectural energetics by Gonlin (1985:95) but was again erroneously presented as

$$\text{Output} = \frac{L}{(Q \times H)} \times (^1/_v + {}^1/_{v'}).$$

The formula used in the present analysis is that of Aaberg and Bonsignore (1975), as cited earlier. One can hope that it will be consistently used by researchers conducting energetic analyses.

Some additional information is necessary to use the transport formula. The value of Q, at least in the present analysis, is assumed to be 22 kg per trip; since Q is expressed as a volume (m^3), each material transported must be converted to volume equivalent to 22 kg. For tuff, 1 m^3 weighs 1,836 kg; thus 22 kg equals .01 m^3. This arithmetic conversion, applied to cobbles, earth, and plaster respectively, yields the following volumes: .01 m^3, .02 m^3, and .01 m^3.

Since transport costs are based in part on distance, a brief comment on that subject is necessary. I derived distances in the present analysis based on known locations between the specific loci of construction and raw materials. As stated in Chapter 2, the sources of many raw materials are generally identifiable. Each estimate of distance was measured as the shortest distance to the available material, and elevation or slope was only marginally included in establishing distance.

The standard cost of manufacturing tuff masonry blocks was determined through two timed replicative experiments involving both steel tools and stone tools (Figure 9). In both cases, the tuff was freshly quarried and, in the second case, the workers were given time to practice using the stone tools (Abrams 1984b). Interestingly, it took very little time for these experienced masons to master the slightly different technology. The comparison of times required to cut masonry blocks (involving the facing of five sides of the block) with both sets of tools yielded a ratio of steel to stone of 1:1.5, and the standard cost of manufacturing masonry blocks with stone tools was 1 m^3/11.6 p-d.

The energetic cost of facing cobbles was estimated to be 10 percent of the cost of facing masonry blocks, or 1 m^3/1.16 p-d. This reduction was based

Figure 9. Manufacturing masonry blocks with stone tools

on the fact that the workmanship on cobbles was much cruder and that only one side of the cobble was worked, in contrast to five sides of the tuff.

The standard cost of sculpturing was based on the timed observations of the sculpturing of a range of motifs evident at Copan (Figure 10). Thirteen motifs, ranging in complexity from simple bars and dots to glyphs and faces, were carved by a part-time sculptor from the town of Copan. Using the actual Classic sculpture as a template, the sculptor was able to carve simple motifs (measured in carved surface area) at a rate of 321 cm/p-h and complex motifs at a rate of 89 cm/p-h (Abrams 1984b).

The manufacture of plaster involved several interrelated activities: cutting, transporting, and stacking trees as well as excavating, preparing, and transporting stone. The standard cost of plaster manufacture was derived by combining transport costs, using the formula presented above, with Erasmus' figures on plaster production (1965:290). The standard cost, 1 m³ of plaster/43.9 p-d, assumes production within the open-air method of lime burning described by several scholars (Morris, Charlot, and Morris 1931; Roys 1934; Hyman 1970). This figure is clearly incorrect for Late Classic

Figure 10. Sculpturing

Copan since data indicate that the calcining of limestone for plaster was likely conducted within enclosed kilns (discussed in Chapter 8). However, I have not yet been able to generate energy costs using that system of production and will rely upon the standard cost presented above. This results in an *over-estimate* of the cost of producing plaster since, presumably, enclosed kilns would increase production efficiency.

During the restoration process, it was observed that the placement of crude fill took very little time, and for the bulk of fill (particularly that in the substructural platform) I did not assign any cost. Essentially, the "cost" of depositing large quantities of earth and stone as fill is subsumed in the transport cost. However, it was estimated that 4.8 m³ of fill/p-d could be set in place in those components of the structure that required greater care. This cost was incorporated for the volume of masonry backing extending 10 cm from all walls and platform surfaces. In addition, this same cost was included for 10 cm of every 1 m in substructure height. Thus a platform measuring 6 m long by 4 m wide by 2 m high involved the cost of placing 8.8 m³ of backing (Table 5). The inclusion of this cost reflects the time necessary for

Table 5. Estimating Volume of Carefully Placed Platform Material

Retaining wall backing = 6 × 2 × .1 (2) = 2.4
Retaining wall backing = 4 × 2 × .1 (2) = 1.6
Intermediate consolidation = 6 × 4 × .1 = 2.4
Platform surface consolidation = 6 × 4 × .1 = 2.4

TOTAL = 8.8 m³

the careful and essential placement of mortar and the added cost of periodic tamping and consolidating of fill. This set of costs was actually quite insignificant, having no effect on either calculations or conclusions.

The standard cost of masonry wall construction was based on timed observations of twenty-one separate instances of constructing such walls as part of the restoration process. It was observed that 3.2 m² of surface area of masonry could be built per p-d or, using a standard masonry wall thickness of .25 m, 0.8 m³ per p-d. This work rate was applied equally to the construction of cobble walls, based on the observed behavioral similarities in the building of these two wall types.

One potential flaw in the standard cost estimate for masonry wall construction is that only the lower portion of the walls was restored; thus I do not have costs for upper wall construction. I imagine that building the upper portions, involving the movement of blocks up to workers on scaffolding, would have been more time-consuming, so my data yield a cost underestimate for this task.

Timed observations of the cobbling of a level surface, serving as the subflooring for plastered surfaces, yielded a standard cost of 9.6 m²/p-d.

I was unable to observe and thus record the time required to plaster surfaces during the restoration process and thus have relied upon a modern estimate for this task. Contemporary estimates for plastering surfaces suggest a rate of 80 m²/p-d (Mahoney 1981:44). This rate of work is based on a plaster thickness of 2.5 cm, and I have not calibrated or applied more specific costs based on plaster thickness. This figure was deemed appropriate based on contextual and behavioral similarities—that is, roughly equivalent physical activities and technology.

The standard costs for the construction of two of the basic components of perishable structures—walls and roofs—as well as *champas,* or wall-less structures, were based primarily on data obtained through a questionnaire survey of fourteen households within the Copan Valley concerning the cost of house construction (Abrams 1984a: Appendix D). A more accurate and simpler version of my original formulae, calculated by Gonlin (1993), represents an improvement in estimating the final cost of house construction and is used in the present work. Gonlin's regression formula is as follows:

$$p\text{-}d = -13.838 + 1.832 \text{ (area)}.$$

For wattle and daub structures, this formula yields a reasonable estimate for procurement, transport, and construction of both the walls and the roof of houses. This, however, does not include the costs associated with the substructural platform. Based on the limited sample of wattle and daub structures from my survey, smaller structures do not fit in this regression equation and thus a minimum of 10 p-d is assigned to the low end of wattle and daub house construction. It is clear that more ethnographic data are required to potentially refine this equation.

The construction cost for *champas* is, unfortunately, even cruder. I took the Gonlin formula for house construction and divided by 10, with a minimum of 1 p-d. Again, this does not include the cost of constructing the platform. This is admittedly arbitrary and, as with house construction, may eventually be refined. I will add, however, that the unit of analysis in the present study is the residence rather than the work platform.

Refinements of Previous Analysis

The set of costs used in previous analyses (Abrams 1984a, 1987, 1989) has been modified in several ways to yield the set of costs used in the present study, the intent being to both simplify and increase the accuracy of the method. First, several relatively minor and insignificant costs—all associated with trees, grass, and water—have been eliminated. For example, in the original assessment of cost in the construction of Structure 10L-22, a large palace in the Main Group, the collective cost of procuring, transporting, and placing water in the construction process was estimated to be 110 p-d out of an original total of 30,499 p-d, or ca. 0.4 percent. Certainly any conclusions based on such an insignificant cost percentage must be further examined. Similarly, the collective cost of cutting and transporting trees, as well as their subsequent manufacture into beams, for that same structure was ca. 37 p-d, or ca. 0.1 percent of the total cost. These small percentages are in fact relatively large compared with their cost in smaller structures. As these very minor costs have no analytic impact on better understanding the Maya, I feel justified in recommending their elimination in any energetic analyses. Second, as discussed above, more accurate formulae for both transport of raw materials and construction of wattle and daub houses have been incorporated. Third, the distance traveled from various loci of construction to sources of earth has been reduced from 1,000 meters, used in my original calculations, to 100 meters for the following reasons: (1) it is likely that earth was procured from the riverine zone in the valley as often as possible, and this zone is close to much of the Late Classic settlement concentrations; (2) house construction, particularly in the foothill zone, would have involved leveling the ground surface, thus effectively serving as a source of ready earth; and (3) it is possible (although as yet unproven) that borrow pits may have existed in relative proximity to major urban barrio construction sites. The effect of this reduction in estimated distance is to lower the transport cost of earth to ca. 10 percent of its original cost. This single modification results in an overall lowering of construction costs since transport is a very costly operation (Abrams 1984a:216, Table 18). The impact of these refinements is represented in Table 6 which gives both the original cost and the revised cost of construction for a sample of buildings. It should be noted that several factors have been altered in this revised method, but certainly those involving the cost of earth transport were most significant.

Table 6. Comparison of Revised Cost Estimate (Minus Reuse) with Original Cost Estimates

Structure	Original Estimate of Cost	Revised Estimate	% Change
10L-22	30,499	24,705	−19
9N-82-C	8,188	8,567	+5
9N-80	1,972	1,903	−7
9M-195-B	5,151	5,058	−2
9M-194-B	2,780	2,761	−1
9M-245-B	295	158	−46
9M-191-N	592	504	−15
9M-191-W	318	191	−40
9M-190	125	72	−42
9M-241	122	98	−20

Source: Abrams 1984a.

Reuse of Construction Materials

Before discussing the structures quantified in this analysis, I must consider one more methodological question—the reuse of building materials. Final structures were commonly built over or expanded from previous, ancestral structures. Similarly, it is well established that buildings located elsewhere and, on occasion, stelae were destroyed specifically to provide new construction material. A central question is how these reused materials are to be quantified in light of the relative ambiguity that surrounds the problem of determining their source and measuring their volume.

The specific method applied to earlier structures was to quantify only those remnants of the structure that were evident and measurable, using the same methods of quantification that were applied to final, more conspicuous episodes of construction. These structures with known volumes of reuse were then quantified, with reuse savings subtracted from the cumulative cost of construction. In addition, all of the structures were quantified assuming no reuse had occurred. Thus some buildings have two costs: (1) the cumulative cost of construction and (2) the final, most costly episode of construction incorporating energy savings from reuse. In the ensuing analyses, the cumulative cost of construction for each residence is used as the unit of analysis in generating relative measures of social power, whereas the reconstruction of labor systems and specialization is based on cumulative cost minus reuse savings.

An alternative method might involve the estimation of the volume of materials in the earlier structure(s) with the assumption that all of the materials in the reconstructed ancestral structure were reused in the later building. I have not used this method for several reasons: (1) doing so would not change the analytic results based on comparative relative costs; (2) I did not feel confident in assuming that I could reconstruct highly destroyed architecture; and (3) I did not want to assume that all of the ancestral build was in fact reused in the final episode of construction. For example, we know that some amount of reused material was incorporated into the construction of Structure 10L-22, a large palace in the East Court of the Main Group. Trik (1939:103), the original excavator, noted that "sculpture and stones found in the fill gave evidence of a razed earlier building, but there was no indication that this had occupied the same site." More recent trenching operations in the East Court indicate that an earlier structure, built in the period A.D. 600–700, underlay Structure 10L-22, which was dedicated in A.D. 715 (Sharer, Miller, and Traxler 1992). Thus it is certain that Structure 10L-22 incorporated some amount of the materials from its structural precursor. The problem, of course, is determining how much of this earlier structure was reused in the construction of Structure 10L-22. Perhaps most of it was; if so, how do we determine the volume of materials based on the remnants of this razed and buried structure? On the other hand, this structure may have been razed for reuse on a completely different construction project. In addition, I lack data concerning the cost of demolition. Thus, in the method used here I generate a single cumulative cost of construction for all structures that errs on the side of cautious overestimation as well as a second cost in those cases where reused materials were evident, measurable, and quantifiable. Certainly future researchers could justifiably explore various alternative approaches that might incorporate possible ancestral structures more completely. In fact, I would argue that alternative methods for quantifying similar structures would help determine perhaps the most effective methodological course in considering reuse.

The Sample of Quantified Structures

The majority of structures quantified in this analysis (Figures 11–14) were those excavated by PAC II; thus "sampling" was de facto predetermined by that research design (Sanders 1986b). From the total set of fully excavated structures at Copan as of 1990, a sample of approximately 36 percent of structures within the urban areas and approximately 40 percent of rural structures was quantified, influenced by various factors. First, any structures whose architectural data were unreported or unavailable to me were necessarily eliminated. Second, structures that were especially complex in the number of construction episodes or that had undergone extensive looting or destruction were excluded. Third, structures not assigned to the Late Classic period were eliminated. Finally, two courtyards in Group 9N-8—D and H—were not included in the quantified sample.

The resultant sample of sixty-one construction episodes—either complete buildings or architecturally distinct components of single buildings—was quantified using the method detailed above. The buildings selected cut across the total range of social statuses evident at Late Classic Copan. Table 7 provides information on each structure, including estimated cumulative cost of construction, place within the Willey-Leventhal typology, and construction materials for the three primary components—the platform, the superstructure, and the roof. To ensure that the analysis represented the widest spectrum of social statuses and work efforts, structures from all categories of architectural complexity, according to the Willey-Leventhal typology, were included. Structures in the present sample range from the simplest perishable

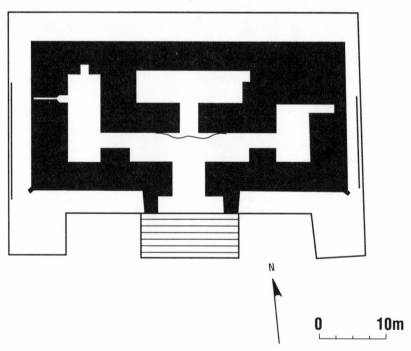

Figure 11. Structure 10L-22: *a*, shown from the East Court; *b*, plan view
(modified from Hohmann and Vogrin 1982)

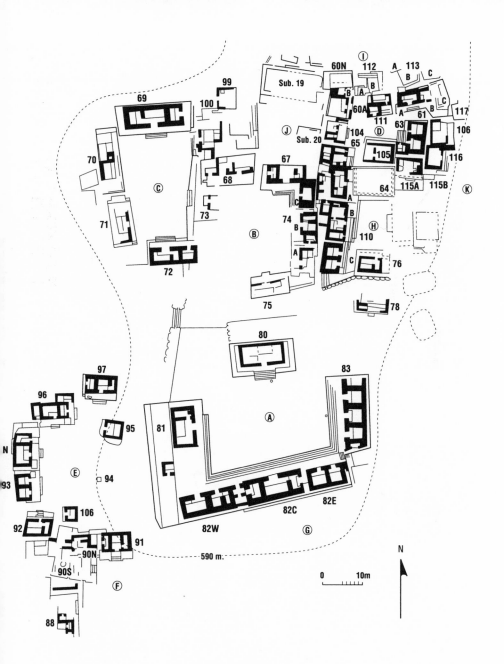

Figure 12. Group 9N-8
(from Webster 1989, with permission from Dumbarton Oaks and the author)

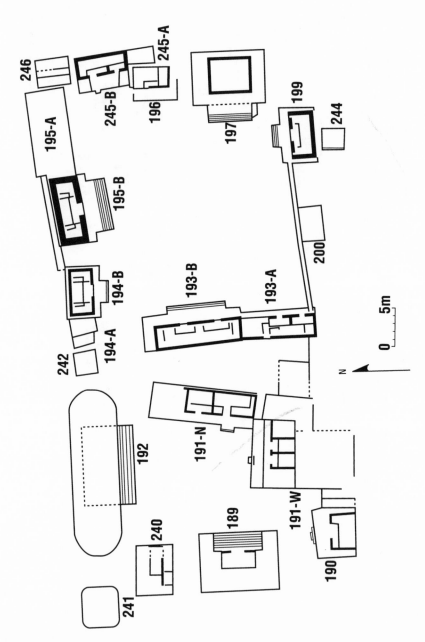

Figure 13. Groups 9M-22A and 9M-22B (modified from Webster 1989)

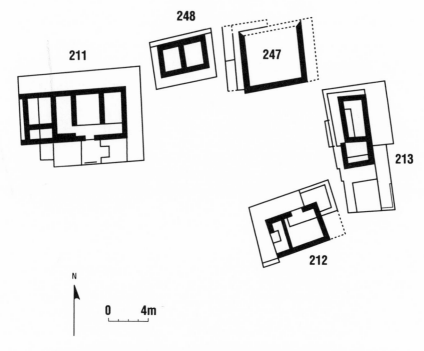

Figure 14. Group 9M-24 (redrawn from Gonlin 1985)

buildings, work platforms, and modest storage facilities to one of the larger palaces in the Main Group—Structure 10L-22. The major gap in quantified structures currently exists for buildings within the Main Group, and future quantitative research should focus on far more structures, construction episodes, and, if possible, reuse within that zone.

Currently, the upper end of the energetic scale is represented by Structure 10L-22, identified as a palace and thus appropriate in any comparative analysis of residential architecture (Trik 1939). More recent epigraphic research has identified this structure with the thirteenth ruler of Copan, 18 Rabbit, who had this structure dedicated in A.D. 715 (Fash 1991a:26; Sharer, Miller, and Traxler 1992:156). A large sample of structures was quantified from the urban barrio of Las Sepulturas, described in various architectural reports (Webster and Abrams 1983; Sanders 1986b, 1990; Webster, Fash, and Abrams 1986; Diamanti 1991; Hendon 1991; Sheehy 1991). Finally, the lower scale is represented by Type 1 structures in Las Sepulturas but principally in the outlying rural zones of the Copan Valley (Gonlin 1985, 1993; Webster and Gonlin 1988).

Table 7. Cumulative Energy Cost per Major Construction Episode

Structure	Cost (p-d)	Function[a]	Type
Main Group			
10L-22	24,705	Residence A	5
Group 9N-8A			
9N-82-C	10,686	Residence A	4
9N-82-E	7,491	Residence A	4
9N-82-W	2,361	Residence C	4
9N-83	5,893	Residence B	4
9N-81	1,007	Residence D/E	4
9N-81-terrace	1,536	Addition	4
9N-81-sub-1	769	Residence F	4
9N-81-sub-2	1,052	Work platform	4
9N-80	2,259	Temple	4
Group 9M-22A			
9M-195-B	5,058	Residence A	3
9M-195-A	160	Work platform	3
9M-194-B	2,761	Residence A	3
9M-194-A	39	Work platform	3
9M-193-B	772	Residence F	3
9M-193-A	422	Residence F	3
9M-199	2,861	Residence A	3
9M-197	1,703	Temple	3
9M-200	30	Entry building	3
9M-242	18	Storage	3
9M-244	20	Work platform	3
9M-245-A	11	Kitchen	3
9M-245-B	214	Residence F	3
9M-246	105	Residence F	3
9M-196	101	Residence F	3
Group 9M-22B			
9M-189	986	Residence D/F	2
9M-191-N	504	Residence F	2
9M-192	452	Unknown	2
9M-191-W	191	Residence F	2
9M-240	92	Residence F	2
9M-241	98	Work platform	2
9M-190	72	Residence F	2
Group 9N-8B			
9N-67	4,477	Residence A	4
9N-73	3,429	Residence B	4
9N-68	2,199	Residence C	4
9N-74-B	2,424	Residence A	4

Table 7. (*continued*)

Structure	Cost (p-d)	Function[a]	Type
9N-74-C	2,297	Residence A	4
9N-74-A	1,988	Residence B	4
9N-75	266	Residence D/F	4
Group 9N-8C			
9N-69	4,021	Residence A	4
9N-72	2,228	Residence B	4
9N-71	1,495	Residence B	4
Group 9N-8E			
9N-97	3,890	Residence A	4
9N-92	256	Residence F	4
9N-95	39	Kitchen	4
9N-108	31	Storage	4
Group 9N-8F			
9N-91	1,665	Residence C	4
Group 9M-24			
9M-212	127	Residence D/F	1
9M-213-A	76	Residence F	1
9M-213-B	20	Residence F	1
Site 30-7			
30-27	29	Residence F	1
30-28	67	Residence F	1
30-29-1	40	Residence F	1
Site 7D-6-2			
Structure 1	32	Residence F	1
Structure 2	71	Residence F	1
Structure 3	21	Kitchen	1
Site 7D-3-1			
Structure 1	37	Residence F	1
Structure 2	23	Residence F	1
Site 11D-11-2			
Structure 1	42	Residence F	1
Structure 1-sub	53	Residence F	1
Structure 2	45	Residence F	1

Note: Cumulative energy cost is the sum of costs per structure from Appendices A and B.

[a]Residence Categories: A = masonry platform, masonry superstructure, vaulted roof; B = masonry platform, masonry superstructure, beam and mortar roof; C = masonry platform, masonry superstructure, grass roof; D = masonry platform, wattle and daub superstructure; E = masonry platform, cobble superstructure; F = cobble platform, wattle and daub superstructure.

A few final comments concerning the present method and application of architectural energetics are in order. Empirical support for the credibility of architectural energetics comes from the fact that rather simple, archaeologically known wattle and daub structures, when quantified, conform quite well with costs of similar structures described in the ethnographic literature. For example, the ethnographic data concerning perishable house construction (summarized in Chapter 7) display a range of costs from ca. 10 to more than 100 p-d. The method used to quantify the archaeological wattle and daub structures yields a similar range, and thus the ethnographic record provides some baseline validity for the quantified costs. As structures in the archaeological record become more complex, the costs increase. Unfortunately, we cannot observe the complete construction of a large Maya palace and thus we have no comparable means of grounding our higher figures. Nonetheless, there does appear to be a logical continuum of costs.

Further justification of the present method of quantification lies in its scientific nature: it is replicable, explicit, comparative, and empirical. I would never suggest that the costs produced are absolutes, and it would be pretentious and misguided for anyone to do so. Rather, these are working figures in a dynamic process of quantification, and I have been quite explicit in highlighting those costs that must be refined. As stated at the beginning of this chapter, the critical goal in the energetic study of architecture is to eliminate by some order of magnitude simplistic and subjective assessments of scale. This methodology is such an attempt. Just as refinements have been made over the past few years, further refinements are expected, thus aligning this method with all others within the domain of science.

5

Costs and the Construction Process

The costs of the quantified structures are of analytic value as empirical measures in the assessment of competing analogs necessary in reconstructing and interpreting Classic Maya institutions. More directly, however, they provide insights into the construction of architectural forms in the sense that cost has an immediate effect on decisions within the building process. In this chapter, I present some descriptive aspects of construction from the perspective of cost.

Comparison of Basic and Improved Residential Structures

For analytic purposes, I have created six different categories of architectural quality, five of which conform to either the basic or improved form (see Table 8). Categories A, B, and C are classified as improved forms, and all have a masonry substructure and masonry superstructure. The distinction among these three categories is in the roof type, with A bearing a vaulted roof, B a beam and mortar roof, and C a grass roof. Categories D and F are basic forms, consisting of a wattle and daub superstructure. The distinction here lies in the quality of the substructural retaining wall, with D having masonry walls and F having roughly shaped cobble walls. Category E comprised those structures with a masonry substructure and cobble-walled superstructure. This category was more hypothetical than real in my sample since only one structure (Structure 9N-81) partially fit within this category.

The first descriptive statistic involves an energetic comparison of basic and improved residential structures, summarized in Table 8. Based on the

Table 8. Comparison of Costs of Residential Categories

Improved Residential Structures (Categories A, B, and C)
  Mean cost of all structures (including 10L-22): 4,839 p-d (91,939/19)
  Mean cost of all structures (excluding 10L-22): 3,735 p-d (67,234/18)
  Modal cost of all improved structures: 2,861 p-d

Basic Residential Structures (Categories D and F)
  Mean cost of all structures: 207 p-d (5,392/26)
  Mean cost of all structures in Las Sepulturas: 310 p-d (4,953/16)
  Mean cost of all structures outside Las Sepulturas: 44 p-d (439/10)
  Modal cost of basic structures in Las Sepulturas = 203 p-d
  Modal cost of basic structures outside Las Sepulturas = 41 p-d
  Modal cost of all basic structures: 96 p-d

cumulative costs of construction, the mean cost of all basic structures (Residential forms D and F) was 207 p-d (5,392/26). The mean cost of basic structures in Las Sepulturas was 310 p-d (4,953/16), whereas the mean cost of basic structures outside the concentrated urban zone was 44 p-d (439/10). The modal cost of all basic structures was 96 p-d. The range of costs for basic structures (not considering isolated building episodes) ranged from 23 p-d for Structure 7D-3-1-2 to 986 p-d for Structure 9M-189.

In contrast, the mean cost for the improved form (Residential forms A, B, and C) was 4,839 p-d (91,939/19). Excluding Structure 10L-22, the mean cost was 3,735 p-d (67,234/18). The modal cost for all improved residential structures was 2,861. Additionally, improved costs ranged from a low of 1,495 p-d for Structure 9N-71 to a high of 24,705 p-d for Structure 10L-22.

From the above comparison of mean costs between the two general house forms, as well as a scrutiny of costs in Tables 7 and 8 and Appendix A, it is clear that there is considerable variation in energy expenditure between these two forms. The critical cost responsible for this variation at Copan is the high cost of *dressed masonry* and, by association, plaster. Tables 9 and 10 present, for each structure, the cost of procuring (quarrying), transporting, and manufacturing tuff for masonry blocks as well as the cost of manufacturing, transporting, and applying plaster to masonry structures; the costs are represented as percentages of the total cost. The mean cost of masonry for all structures in the sample was 49 percent. The mean cost of masonry for improved structures was 73 percent, while that for basic structures (essentially expended in the platform) was 20 percent. Plaster for all structures in the

Table 9. Percentage of Costs per Operation for Each Structure

Structure	Pro-curement	Transport	Manu-facture	Con-struction	Tuff[a]	Plaster[b]
10L-22	11	41	45	3	39	28
9N-82C	9	49	39	4	65	30
9N-82E	8	48	41	3	63	31
9N-82W	10	53	33	4	84	12
9N-83	9	50	36	4	60	28
9N-81	10	40	18	33	40	9
9N-81-terrace	14	57	26	4	63	10
9N-81-sub-1	11	55	29	5	66	13
9N-81-sub-2	14	57	25	4	52	13
9N-80	9	34	40	16	51	20
9M-195B	10	50	36	4	68	18
9M-195A	15	41	0	43	0	0
9M-194B	9	48	39	4	63	26
9M-194A	13	51	15	21	0	0
9M-193B	7	52	11	30	0	8
9M-193A	7	49	16	28	0	13
9M-199	10	48	38	4	68	22
9M-197	12	51	23	14	52	12
9M-200	13	53	9	25	0	0
9M-242	1	26	26	42	0	0
9M-244	14	38	1	45	0	0
9M-245A	9	55	9	27	0	0
9M-245B	5	39	21	34	23	18
9M-246	4	25	15	56	0	19
9M-196	6	41	19	34	0	32
9M-189	10	56	27	5	61	10
9M-191N	8	57	25	21	28	21
9M-192	10	57	2	32	0	3
9M-191W	9	59	17	16	0	17
9M-240	9	30	3	58	0	4
9M-241	5	36	10	48	0	4
9M-190	11	57	3	29	0	0
9N-67	11	55	31	3	87	8
9N-73	9	52	36	3	71	21
9N-68	11	55	31	3	83	9
9N-74B	11	54	31	3	85	6
9N-74C	9	50	39	3	64	28

Table 9. (*continued*)

Structure	Pro-curement	Transport	Manu-facture	Con-struction	Tuff[a]	Plaster[b]
9N-74A	11	56	30	3	82	8
9N-75	9	43	27	21	45	19
9N-69	11	54	32	3	80	12
9N-72	10	53	33	4	80	13
9N-71	11	54	32	3	80	12
9N-97	10	54	34	3	79	16
9N-92	6	25	17	52	0	22
9N-95	9	27	11	57	0	0
9N-108	6	23	29	43	0	37
9N-91	11	55	30	4	88	4
9M-212	13	48	21	18	54	5
9M-213A	14	48	13	25	42	0
9M-213B	8	17	4	71	0	0
30-27	10	31	7	53	0	0
30-28	8	27	5	61	0	0
30-29	14	23	11	52	0	0
7D-6-2-1	18	30	3	48	0	0
7D-6-2-2	11	24	5	61	0	0
7D-6-2-3	10	24	5	62	0	0
7D-3-1-1	12	29	7	51	0	0
7D-3-1-2	8	23	4	65	0	0
11D-11-2-1	11	26	7	56	0	0
11D-11-2-1-sub	16	33	7	44	0	0
11D-11-2-2	15	33	8	44	0	0

Note: Percentages are based on cumulative cost estimates.

[a] Includes all costs associated with the procurement, transport, and manufacture of masonry blocks.

[b] Includes all costs associated with the transport, manufacture, and application of plaster.

sample averaged 15 percent of the total cost of construction; the mean for improved structures and basic structures was 17 percent and 13 percent, respectively. Masonry buildings at Copan (and all other Maya sites) were necessarily plastered, and the mean collective costs associated with both masonry and plaster on average for all improved structures was 90 percent of total cost. It is thus clear that the huge cost involving masonry was the key energetic distinction between basic and improved house forms. This high

Table 10. Summary of Cost Percentages

Operations for All Structures (N = 61)
  Procurement: 615/61 = 10%
  Transport: 2,629/61 = 43%
  Manufacture: 1,247/61 = 20%
  Construction: 1,617/61 = 27%

Operations for Improved Structures (Residential Categories A, B, C; N = 19)
  Procurement: 191/19 = 10%
  Transport: 982/19 = 52%
  Manufacture: 666/19 = 35%
  Construction: 65/19 = 3%
  Expenditures relating to masonry: 1,389/19 = 73%
  Expenditures relating to plaster: 332/19 = 17%

Operations for Basic Structures within Las Sepulturas (Residential Categories D and F; N = 16)
  Procurement: 137/16 = 9%
  Transport: 701/16 = 44%
  Manufacture: 268/16 = 17%
  Construction: 503/16 = 31%
  Expenditures relating to masonry (all absorbed in platform construction): 319/16 = 20%
  Expenditures relating to plaster: 201/16 = 13%

Operations for Basic Structures outside Las Sepulturas (N = 10)
  Procurement: 123/10 = 12%
  Transport: 279/10 = 28%
  Manufacture: 64/10 = 6%
  Construction: 535/10 = 54%
  Expenditures relating to masonry and plaster: 0%

cost of masonry is also the key factor in the energetic ranking of roof types. The least costly roof type is certainly the grassed or thatched roof; a beam and mortar roof is more costly, followed by the vaulted form. This cost continuum is directly related to the volume of masonry and plaster required by each roof type.

This distinction in form and energy is also reflected in the comparison of costs per operation (Tables 8 and 9). The improved form absorbed the most energy during the transport and manufacture operations, again reflecting the high cost of masonry. The mean costs of transport and manufacture for the improved form were 52 percent and 35 percent, respectively, of the total cost of construction. These percentages drop to 44 percent and 17 percent, respectively, for basic structures in Las Sepulturas and to 28 percent and 6 percent, respectively, for basic structures in the rural zone. This differential in the relative costs of transport and manufacture is reflected in the relative cost of construction, or assembly, which increases from 3 percent in improved structures to 54 percent in basic structures. Interestingly, the relative cost of procurement of materials changed very little in the comparison of structural forms.

The Building Process

It is assumed that the Maya builders were cognizant of the relative energy expenditures in the various components of architecture. The generation of cost estimates then allows for a consideration of the building process from the perspective of costs. In the following analysis I will consider only the improved form, and the reader is referred to Robert Wauchope's (1938) ethnographic research for a discussion of the construction of the basic form, upon which I cannot improve.

The Platform. The platform, which I equate with the substructure, is composed of two basic components that involve construction activities—the core or fill and the outer retaining surface, whether it be a floor surface, a terrace, steps, or a simple retaining wall. The fill at Copan is a combination of rocks and earth, with the percentage of rocks increasing as the size of the superstructure increases. The projected weight of the finished superstructure undoubtedly encouraged the incorporation of greater weight-bearing materials through the increased use of rocks. The cost of rocks or cobbles is greater than that of earth, principally in terms of transport rather than procurement, although the differential is not extreme.

The construction of the fill was a combination of random and nonrandom placement of earth and rocks. My impression is that placement was often influenced by timing—by and large, the work party that happened to arrive dumped that particular material in place. In larger structures, a more conscious effort to strategically distribute and pack material was required, and I have included this added time to consolidate the fill in my calculations of cost (see Chapter 4), thus incorporating the cost of those nonrandom acts associated with the platform fill. In addition to earth and stone, water was episodically added to the fill for the purpose of packing the earth and making the mortar. Although the cost of tamping and consolidating the substructural fill (as fine fill) was incorporated, it was low and not very useful. The cost of procuring and transporting water was so minor that it was not included in these calculations.

The mortar used to bind the fill with the exterior surface was mud rather than the lime-based mortar found in improved structures at other sites (Pollock 1965). *Sascab,* or decomposed limestone, used in mortar at many other Maya sites, was not used in the manufacture of mortar or plaster at Copan, despite the fact that it is present at Copan and would have reduced to some degree the actual manufacturing cost of plaster. This decision was likely affected by consideration of availability, abundance, and location, all of which influence cost. In the Copan Valley today, the closest source of *sascab* is about 12 km from the Main Group, and it is possible that, in part, the high transport cost inhibited the selection of *sascab* in the construction process. The use of a weak mortar at Copan would have then placed greater importance on both protecting the structure with plaster and carefully distributing the weight of the load of the superstructure. More so than mortar, it was the stones themselves that had to bear the weight of the load. Since dressed masonry can be placed in a more direct vertical plane, these walls can bear greater weight than cobble walls, more effectively preventing vertical force from being transformed into lateral force.

As was noted by Pollock (1965:398), many improved structures were built over previous structures, providing greater stability and strength to the fill or core of the final building. The razing and reuse of structures, which left intact the base of the substructure, supplied both necessary materials for the final construction and specific supports for the new superstructure. Task walls or footings were often built in the platform fill directly under that spot expected to bear the greatest weight of the superstructure. If no previous substructure existed, these supports—essentially the nonrandom placement of earth and stone—often had to be built. The absence of a previous substructure would have added cost both in terms of the lack of ready fill material and especially the lack of reusable masonry. In fact, there would have been a great incentive, strictly in terms of reuse savings, to build over earlier structures, and perhaps to some degree these savings contributed to the continuity in specific habitation loci by the Maya.

Many excavators of large masonry structures have made the observation that reused materials constituted part of the substructural as well as superstructural walls (e.g., Satterthwaite 1954). As just one case in point, the substructural retaining walls of Structure 9M-245-B are one-third dressed masonry and two-thirds rough-cut cobbles. Why, we may ask, did the builders use different qualities and types of stones? My answer is that they looted masonry from another building, which provided only one-third of the necessary material for completion of the substructure (see Appendix B). The remainder of the walls were built of the less costly cobbles, with a coating of plaster appropriately masking the difference in quality. Different types of building materials may indicate reuse, and a careful recording of each stone type in a structure may further our assessment and thus methodological control of reuse.

The cost of building the substructure can also be considered from the perspective of expansion. During the use-life of many masonry structures, the substructure was expanded horizontally or vertically or both for a variety of reasons: increased need for activity space, structural reinforcement, status expression, and so forth. In terms of cost, the horizontal expansion was relatively minor since this expansion had no impact on the superstructure itself and many of the materials in the now underlying substructure could be reused. Specifically, the upper portions of the retaining wall were often removed and reused in construction of the larger wall. Vertical expansion of the substructure, however, required a series of modifications of the superstructure and effectively precluded reuse of substructural materials. Thus, from an energetic perspective, it was "cheaper" to extend out than to build up.

Construction of either a new or expanded platform also involved the secondary deposition of refuse. One important benefit of platform construction was that it provided sealed space in which refuse could be eliminated. I am not suggesting that platforms were built in order to provide such space, any more than I would suggest that crawl spaces in contemporary houses in the United States are built to facilitate the deposition of construction debris. Nonetheless, one of the consequences of platform construction and expansion was the effective removal of refuse or the sealing of middens. Parenthetically, accumulations of tuff chips in the platform fill not only support this secondary role of the fill as a repository of discard, but further indicate that the manufacture of masonry was conducted simultaneously with the construction of the platform fill.

Superstructure. Archaeologists' long history of studying masonry structures has yielded considerable knowledge of the engineering skills of the Maya, a fact established very early in the history of Maya archaeology (Roys 1934). Since the construction of the superstructure took considerable care and design, we can presume that the builders had "a previously perfected guide" to direct construction (Pollock 1965:395) as well as a set of tools and units of measurement. Through careful ethnohistoric and ethnographic research, archaeologists have cogently argued that the ancient Maya would have had standard units of measurement for use in the design and construction of masonry buildings (O'Brien and Christiansen 1986). Various construction tools have been identified archaeologically (Andrews IV and Rovner 1973; Lewenstein 1987; Eaton 1991). Certainly a more complete set of construction tools existed, such as a plumb, a leveling tool comparable to the Roman chorobate, and a surveying instrument perhaps comparable to the Roman groma. Thus far, the evidence we have for superstructural building guides are some black lines found under a wall of the A-V Complex (Construction H) at Uaxactun (Smith 1950:24) and possibly several incised lines on a plaster floor at El Mirador (Matheny 1980:34–35).

There does exist some uncertainty regarding the care that went into superstructural assembly at Copan. Trik (1939:95), for example, noted that the masons who built Structure 10L-22 did not break, or alternate, joints between courses of masonry except at certain corners. Pollock (1965:404) stated that "the lack of breaking of joints and of bonding, except at salient corners . . . , were weaknesses common to virtually all Maya masonry." This would seem to contradict basic architectural design, especially at Copan, since, given the very weak mud mortar, the structural integrity (and thus longevity) of the walls depended heavily on careful bonding of corners and breaking of joints. Therefore, I examined photographs of several superstructures at Copan and calculated the percentage of broken joints and bonded corners. I found that between 80 percent and 90 percent of the joints on the front superstructure wall of the *restored* Structure 10L-22 were in fact broken. This same exercise was conducted on several of the masonry structures in Las Sepulturas, restored with extreme accuracy by Rudy Larios V. The percentage of broken joints ranged from 75 percent to 95 percent, again reflecting the concern of the Maya architect in trying to prevent structural failure. Interestingly, one of the indices of distinct construction episodes is the lack of broken joints, indicative of a previous edge of the building. If these were eliminated from my estimates, the percentage of broken joints would be even higher.

When scrutinizing courses of masonry, it should be remembered that these masonry blocks were individually made and that considerable variation in dimensions exists. This variation is caused in part by the stone itself—it is quite soft when freshly quarried and easily breaks. As discussed in Chapter 4, about 50 percent of the quarried stone is removed in the manufacture of the masonry block, and most of this waste ends up in the fill. In addition, variation is caused by differences in the masons' skill and the opportunism of the builders, using earlier materials when available, with their "flaws" simply hidden under a coat of plaster.

Various other aspects of construction of the superstructure deserve mention. The wooden lintels spanning archways had to be extremely hard and dense in order to bear the weight of the walls and roof. Recent excavation of Structure 10L-22A, adjacent to 10L-22, yielded the remains of a wooden lintel made of just such a wood, identified as *chicozapote* (B. Fash et al. 1992:427). Furthermore, a careful examination and reconstruction of the facade of Structure 9N-82C indicated that the sculptured blocks were carved in place on the building rather than sculptured on the ground and then assembled (Fash 1991a), a logical procedure given the complexity of the design. The analysis of wall type and especially wall thickness to determine probable roof type, perhaps first conducted at Piedras Negras by Linton Satterthwaite (1954), has been conducted by Sanders (1989) at Copan and is our best measure of roof type in those cases lacking sufficient direct evidence. Incrementally, these analyses greatly add to our understanding of the decisions made by the Maya concerning the process of construction.

In terms of construction, damage to the walls or the roofs would have required removal and reconstruction of these components. In terms of cost, this process would not have been particularly costly; on the other hand, it certainly would have been wise and presumably desired by the occupant to protect the building in as many ways as possible. These structures had to withstand the various forces of entropy that acted against the initial energy expenditure, the primary entropic force being heavy seasonal rain. One obvious means of providing greater protection would have been to simply slope the roof, thus minimizing the dual stresses of the direct impact of rainfall and the weight of standing rainwater on the roof. Certainly the Maya architect was capable of employing through design this rather simple but effective technique; given the fact that masonry structures evolved from wattle and daub structures, which have gabled roofs, it seems reasonable to assume that this same principle for water movement would have been employed on masonry structures. In fact, de Landa (Tozzer 1941:86) noted that the roofs of elite houses were sloped, likely for protection against the sun and the rain. Many archaeologists, however, overlook this feature in reconstructing roofs (e.g., Webster and Abrams 1983). Pollock (1965:400, Fig. 14) presents only one drawing—a beam and mortar roof at Tulum excavated by Samuel Lothrop—exhibiting a sloped roof. Direct evidence of a sloping roof has been recovered from the excavations at Copan. In the collapse behind Structure 9N-82C, two large sections of plaster from the roof were recovered. The surfaces of both of these demonstrated a clear incline, indicating that water was perceived as a problem and its removal was being addressed. Even more compelling, drainage stones were found in the same context, clearly indicating that water was being channeled from the roof (Webster, Fash, and Abrams 1986:171). Even without drainage stones, large masonry structures could have been built with sloped roofs simply and inexpensively by sloping the plaster finish rather than varying the height of the walls. Our portrayal of masonry roofs as level, coupled with our occasional manufacture of 90-degree angles, is perhaps a product of our own cultural environment rather than anything intended by the Maya.

Sloping roofs may have had additional benefits for the occupants of Maya courtyards. During the rainy season, a considerable amount of erosion occurs on the foothills, soiling the Copan River. Paradoxically, the rainy season may have been a time of potable water shortages in river valleys. Perhaps springs were an important supplemental source of potable water during this season, as they are in Copan today. Another possibility, however, is that sloped roofs may have been used as devices to capture water during the rainy season. Forde (1963:152–153), for example, in his description of Yoruba courtyards, stated, "The rain-water flowing from the inner slopes of the roofs, especially where it is concentrated at the corners of the compound, is caught in large pottery butts and used for household purposes." Thus, hypothetically, sloped roofs may have served the dual purposes of water removal and capture. The importance of water capture in citywide planning has been demonstrated for Tikal (Scarborough and Gallopin 1991).

The final set of activities relating to construction involves the manufacture and application of plaster to both the platform and superstructure. The cost of using lime-based plaster (i.e., in transport and manufacture) was reasonably high; as stated, the costs associated with plaster for masonry structures subsumed on average 17 percent of the total cost of the structure. Despite this high cost, plaster was an essential component of construction in protecting the structure. Once the tropical rains penetrated or eroded the plaster, the walls lost their strength, placing the stability of the entire superstructure in jeopardy. The need for plaster was continuous, and its production was annual yet seasonal. It must also be recognized that plaster is unique among building materials in that it cannot be reused (David Hyman, personal communication, 1988). Once plaster is set, it cannot be unset. Plaster production is discussed in detail in Chapter 8.

Courtyards were also part of the construction domain. A relatively level earthen surface was first prepared and fill was set in place, covered first by a subsurface of grouting and then by the plaster itself. The cost of courtyards was dependent upon the volume of the courtyard as a construction feature, the thickness of the plaster, and, in the largest of compounds, the presence of architecture targeted for demolition and burial. In most cases, the cost of greatest consequence was associated with initial plastering and subsequent replastering. The costs associated with plaster far outweigh those associated with procurement and transport of earth and cobbles, the principal components in the fill. The grouting material is often nothing more than tuff chips from construction or reused materials. In addition, after a courtyard is constructed, it tends to be maintained (i.e., replastered) rather than destroyed for new courtyard construction. Since plaster was in essence the only manufactured material in courtyard construction, the overall cost of construction of this architectural feature was low relative to the costs of associated residential structures. As a corollary, the low cost of courtyards relative to that of residential structures justifies the use of the latter as the more informative unit of analysis in the present work.

A final aspect of the construction of courtyards is drainage and slope. Although often drawn as perfectly level, enclosed courtyards at Copan were invariably sloped to allow for water drainage, as is evidenced at Tikal (Scarborough and Gallopin 1991). Hendon (1991) has demonstrated that courtyard surfaces were used for a variety of domestic activities. Having the courtyard fill with water each day during the rainy season hardly makes sense. Similarly, standing water on the plastered courtyard surface would only have hastened its erosion, thus increasing the maintenance cost. Lentz (1991:283) has recently suggested that useful trees may have existed in and around courtyards at Copan, and perhaps in addition to simply sloping the courtyard surface, central areas of courtyards were left unplastered, reserved for trees or some other natural foliage to absorb runoff.

Maintenance Costs

The quantification of maintenance costs is important in that it (1) provides insights in reconstructing behaviors and organization regarding the complete construction process; (2) provides the necessary energetic data to assess the relation between the cost of initial construction and that of repair; and

(3) more completely defines the appropriate units of analysis. If, for example, the cost of *annual* repair of buildings was greater than that of initial construction, then those repair cost estimates would be the more appropriate comparative figures. Although I have not tried to calculate maintenance costs per se for structures, these costs can be derived from the breakdown of construction costs, repair being largely subsumed in the cost associated with plaster. With this in mind, the cost of any single act of maintenance should be rather low relative to the initial cost of construction. The cumulative cost of multiple, long-term repairs would be very difficult to incorporate since estimating these figures requires considerable knowledge of the presence, timing, and extent of repair, aspects of construction that are often difficult to ascertain archaeologically. After scrutinizing the buildings in my sample and calculating their respective cost of construction, I decided that the most informative energetic units of analysis in the present study are the cumulative cost of construction and the cost of construction of the largest, final building episode.

A final thought concerning maintenance involves its relation to initial construction. McGuire and Schiffer (1983:282) state that "usually low maintenance cost is achieved by greater manufacturing cost, and low manufacturing cost tends to inflate the cost of maintenance." The authors suggest that the ability to spend more during initial construction, which then results in savings in the long term, is one economic benefit of the elite in the context of increasing inequality. These authors are in fact correct when considering *similar* categories of architecture. Improved masonry structures, for example, built with higher-quality blocks or larger quantities of plaster, will save on later repair costs. However, when we compare the costs of *dissimilar* structures, such as improved versus basic residences, the above relationship does not necessarily apply. Improved structures contain so many more components and costs that even the repair of these structures exceeds the initial cost of constructing a basic residence. For example, the cost involved in plastering Structure 9N-82C was estimated to be 2,568 p-d. If in a single year only 20 percent, say, of the structure required replastering, that would still cost roughly 514 p-d. By comparison, the initial cost of building a basic wattle and daub dwelling was generally less than 100 p-d. I believe this qualification holds true in the contemporary world; I would not be surprised to find that the annual costs of maintaining the expensive homes or compounds of the elite in the United States today far surpass the cost of maintaining (or perhaps even buying) a home for many other citizens.

6

Energetics and the Hierarchy of Social Power

The energetic costs of architecture at Copan, generated through the methodology described in Chapter 4, serve as the basis for analyses of various aspects of Classic Maya society. The most immediate characteristic of Maya society to be addressed is its general sociopolitical hierarchy, a topic prominent in Maya studies since at least the work of Morley (1946). The importance of first establishing the sociopolitical hierarchy rests on the fact that the macro-level structure of social and political power relations is the most direct and logical inference derived from the energetic data and that it provides the necessary anthropological springboard for ensuing interpretations. We cannot discuss, say, economic activities without first accepting some broad model of the sociopolitical structure as best approximated for the Maya state from these or other data.

It is proposed that the comparative cumulative energetic costs expended in the construction of only residential architecture serve as the best index of the hierarchic structure of social status and political power for the Late Classic Maya. The use of energy differentials in residential structures as general measures of status and power is supported by several factors. First, there is a powerful logical argument that links high status and power with concomitant levels of energy expenditure in residences predicated upon the differential ability to amass the requisite labor for such distinct construction projects. Second, as presented in Chapter 3, more costly residential structures offer their occupants a distinctly higher biopsychological quality of life, which within a state system is associated with high power and status. Third, independent glyphic, mortuary, ceramic, and architectural studies all conclude that more costly architecture is associated with high levels of social power (Sanders 1989; Webster 1989; Sheehy 1991; Hendon 1991; Fash and Stuart 1991; Diamanti 1991). Finally, there is an enormous corpus of ethnographic literature that supports the general connection between status and architecture. This association, for example, was observed for the sixteenth century Yucatecan Maya (Tozzer 1941:62). Helms (1979:9) sees the larger, more complex, and better-quality houses of sixteenth-century Panamanian chiefs as "overt evidence of the high status and authority, prestige, and power of the ruler." Statements such as these, pertaining to a wide variety of ranked and stratified societies, make it difficult to ignore the relationship between architecture and social power; in fact, comparative architectural analysis is perhaps one of the best collective means through which archaeologists can infer social and political power relationships.

Power and Status

The notion that architecture may serve as an index of cultural complexity has generally been accepted in social science since the mid-nineteenth century. There are, however, various specific contextual qualifications to this general correlation that affect the archaeological reconstruction of cultural systems, predicated primarily on the fact that power is not equivalent to status in all cultural settings. Status in the political domain is akin to "authority," defined as "the ability to channel the behavior of others in the absence of the use or threat of use of sanctions" (Fried 1967:13). "Power," or social power, refers to "the ability to channel the behavior of others by threat or use of sanctions" (ibid.:13). Similarly, power is the political means through which social inequality is created and maintained (e.g., Adams 1975). Power over people, within the broad structure of society, is ultimately generated through direct or indirect control over essential factors of production, such as land, labor, water, and, in the modern world, capital. Status and power are clearly recognized as interactive and in many cases overlapping; Fried (1967:13), for example, notes that it is indeed rare to find cases in which an individual or social group possesses power without status or authority. The opposite, however, readily exists; there are many cases in which high status does not confer significant measures of power. Celebrities in U.S. society, for example, may have high status with little if any real (i.e., infrastructural) power (Mills 1956). Individuals or families who once possessed high power and status may maintain (perhaps at some cost) their status position without necessarily maintaining comparable access to the control of power. Interestingly, some individuals or families with ready access to power may intentionally deflect "fame" or some other measure of social-status recognition; it is a calculated strategy in the United States that many of those families of greatest social power are completely anonymous to the population at large.

Haviland (1981), for example, has reconstructed just such a case for Group 7F-1 at Tikal. He suggests that, although this group included high-status elite residences, the political power of these individuals was tempered by dynastic change, and this power was not consistent with the high quality of architecture. People do not remove rooms or exterior ornamentation simply to reflect to others a decline in wealth or power. We should bear in mind that the costs of maintaining architecture are relatively low; thus, visually "maintaining" one's status through expenditures in architecture is, at least on a short-term basis, relatively inexpensive. Thus, in any particular case, status need not be equated with power.

A second qualification in assessing the energy cost in architecture is that, in some cases, variations in energy expenditure are simply caused by factors other than status or power. Certainly, the primary factor in this context is the fluctuation in the domestic cycle; essentially, family size will influence house size (e.g., Watson 1978; Wilk 1983; Haviland 1988; Tourtellot 1988b). My own Copan survey data support this to some degree. As just one case in point, an old man with no wife and no coresident offspring built a house for himself with an interior space measuring 9 m^2, well below the average house size. In the present study, it is likely that variations in the energy expended in residential structures, particularly within the relatively egalitarian sector of Maya society, may reflect more the dynamics of household size.

A third qualification involves the association of houses with households. One essential element to the research agenda of "household archaeology" has been to reveal the variety of household forms in both past and present communities, with attempts to detail the architectural signatures of such variation (Wilk and Ashmore 1988). Although excellent work along these lines has been conducted at Tikal (Haviland 1988), Seibal (Tourtellot 1988b), and Copan (Sheehy 1991; Diamanti 1991), this linkage between the social unit and the material reflection of that unit as expressed in architecture is not well defined. Although simple rural dwellings tend to represent monogamous households, with extended families coresiding within courtyards, elite structures and courtyards are more problematic. Polygynous and monogamous households may share the same courtyards, and there may be considerable variation in the degree of generational depth within any courtyard.

Thus, until further analyses clearly identify the specific form of household with specific residential structures, I will simply equate a house with a nuclear household. Future analyses might combine the costs of two or more houses if these structures represent a single household (e.g., the residence of a polygynous male and the residence of the wives within that household).

A final qualification is that this analysis is based on the assumption that all structures were occupied simultaneously; thus, I am ignoring the specific history of construction and occupation of courtyards, treating all Late Classic construction as a single comparative unit. I have chosen this analytic course since the goal is to generate an approximate societywide structure of status and power rather than any single set of power relations within a specific courtyard.

Collectively, architectural energetics alone may not be sufficient to reveal all of the very specific and historic variations in social power. However, architectural energetics, at this preliminary stage of research, will reveal the general relations of social power, thus providing the empirical basis for the comparative analysis of a range of complex political systems.

Models

For several decades, archaeologists have recognized models as an essential component in reconstructing the past. The necessity of sociopolitical models for the prehispanic Maya has been clear. These various anthropological models, offered as general systemic analogs for the Classic Maya, include, either in part or as whole entities, the sixteenth-century Yucatecan Maya states (Fash 1983), contemporary Mayan societies (Wilk 1983), West African kingdoms (Sanders 1976), East African kingdoms (Sanders 1981), feudal Europe (Adams and Smith 1981), feudal Japan (Wilk 1988), and Southeast Asian kingdoms (Coe 1957; Demarest 1991). All of these scholars and those who employ any of these models realize fully that analogs represent questions or hypotheses that must be tested against all available empirical data before they can become conclusive. Furthermore, all recognize that, ultimately, the Maya were not Asians, Africans, or Europeans but rather, in the emic and historic sense, were distinctly Maya. Implicit is the recognition that certain levels of cultural specificity simply cannot be reached given the nature of archaeological data. Nonetheless, the Maya could neither deny the principles governing physics and physiology nor circumvent the human imperative to valuate external physical and social resources, collective principles that provided the foundation for nonrandom and probabilistic decisions by the Maya.

As expected, all of these models represent societies that are historically and in some ways institutionally quite distinct (Diamanti 1991). Rather than address these differences, however, I prefer to focus on their similarities since many share common institutional structures and *in general* (i.e., homogenizing history) are appropriate for the Classic Maya. Specifically, most of these models similarly define and structure sociopolitical relations for the Classic Maya based on accounts of the early states or kingdoms, modeled as the segmentary state (Southall 1991). Although healthy disagreement exists (cf. Chase and Chase 1992), it is generally recognized that the larger Maya states, in terms of degree and distribution of power, were more complex than simple ranked societies. Furthermore, it has long been recognized (Sanders and Price 1968) that the Maya states were far less complex, based on those same criteria, than imperial Teotihuacan and, by inference, various other expansionary empires that controlled hundreds of thousands or even millions of people. Although various terms have been assigned to this general political system, the "early state" is simple and appropriate. Most Mayanists agree that Late Classic Maya sociopolitical units were more similar, in sociopolitical structure and the concept of power, to West African or Southeast Asian kingdoms than to pharaonic Egypt or dynastic China.

A collective description of sociopolitical structures that were instituted as part of these early states, based on the analogs listed above, includes (1) limited centralized control of political power, with power relatively diffuse throughout a hierarchy of political elite; (2) a redundancy of many functions throughout the political hierarchy; (3) power ultimately linked to and dependent upon agricultural productivity, with usufruct serving as the primary mechanism for access to agricultural land; (4) a sociopolitical hierarchy wherein kinship obligations played a dominant role in guiding a wide range of cultural interactions; (5) a hierarchic structure of social corporate units in which individuals were affiliated with and obliged to participate in more than one level of the hierarchy; and (6) control and orchestration of the vast majority of economic production held by these various social corporate units (see also Hammond 1991b:255). Further analogous institutional characteristics include the continued worship of ancestors as a dominant religious practice (Sanders 1989; Fash 1991b) as well as warfare that only episodically led to successful control over other polities (Webster 1977; Demarest 1991).

These general sociopolitical characteristics are further represented in what is termed the "lineage model" of the Classic Maya. Sanders (1989:102) has been most explicit in describing this model, particularly in terms of sociopolitical hierarchic relations. He describes these nested social relations of power as follows: (1) extended family households represent the smallest and most interactive sociopolitical unit; (2) these households are incorporated into "lineages of varying size and generational depth"; (3) the heads of maximal lineages represent each of those separate sociopolitical corporate units, serving various economic, political, social, and religious functions for those groups; and (4) the sociopolitical hierarchy is topped by a king representing both the head of the highest ranking lineage and the head of state. According to this model, elite households would be those that provided administrative or certain economic services within the ranked structure of the lineage and state. Although there would have existed a stratified ruling elite, elite households below the level of maximal lineage head and king would be ranked, with positions of power still determined based on kinship (Sanders 1992: 282). Understandably, the majority of individuals would be classified as nonelites, members of households with relatively limited and equal access to social power.

To date, some empirical evidence from Copan has been offered in support of this model. The spatial distribution of courtyards according to type supports this model to some degree (Freter 1988). Hendon (1991) presents artifactual data that indicate a low level and redundancy of economic specialization, much of which took place within residential courtyards. Furthermore, Hendon argues convincingly that courtyard units contained social corporate groups related by kinship, supported by the extensive mortuary analysis by Storey (1986). The low level of economic specialization is further supported by analyses of ground-stone artifacts (Spink 1983), chipped-stone artifacts (Mallory 1984; Valdez and Potter 1991), and ceramic artifacts (Freter 1991). Finally, glyphic data at Copan also indicate the presence of lineages (Fash and Stuart 1991). The following presentation of energy costs addresses most directly the sociopolitical component of the general model, providing further support for its acceptance.

The Energy Hierarchy

Based on the lineage model as an expression of the early segmentary state, we would expect the energy differentials in architecture to reflect (1) a low percentage of very high levels of energy indicative of the ruling, stratified elite; (2) relatively high yet descending energy costs indicative of the ranked lineage elite; and (3) a very large cluster of low energy reflecting the majority segment of commoners. It is also possible that the presence of a lower cluster of energy, reflecting an underclass, would be part of this early state. As stated, the database that would best reflect the structure of social power at Late Classic Copan is the sample of only *residential* structures and their *cu-*

mulative energy costs. As Arnold and Ford (1980) argued, social power can be best assessed energetically through a comparison of *total* energy expended in architecture; in the present study, residences, as a common functional unit of analysis, are used exclusively. This procedural decision avoids the problem of estimating reuse for all residences in the sample and recognizes that social power is a part of one's cumulative social persona, inherited across generations. As such, a sample of forty-six cases is used, taken from Table 7.

The first analytic step toward reconstructing social power involved conducting a hierarchical cluster analysis using the Ward Method. The dendrogram resulting from this statistical analysis is illustrated in Figure 15. Based on the cumulative costs of residences from the sample of structures quantified, six significantly distinct clusters of energy are revealed.

The cluster with the highest cost contains only Structure 10L-22, at a cost of approximately 25,000 p-d. The second cluster contains Structures 9N-82C and 9N-82E, costing roughly between 7,500 p-d and 11,000 p-d. Structure 9N-82, taken as a single structure, represents the second tier in the hierarchy of social power. The third cluster contains six structures, with energy costs ranging from about 3,500 p-d to 6,000 p-d. Five of these residences are located in Group 9N-8 (Structures 67, 69, 73, 83, and 97); the remaining structure in this cluster—9M-195B—is associated with Group 9M-22A. The fourth cluster contains fourteen structures, with costs ranging roughly from 1,000 p-d to 3,000 p-d. Ten of these structures are in Group 9N-8 (Structures 82W, 74A, 74B, 74C, 72, 68, 71, 81, 91, and 81-sub-1), three are in Group 9M-22A (Structures 194B, 193B, and 199), and one is in Group 9M-22B (Structure 189). The fifth cluster contains ten residences of low energy, ranging from about 100 p-d to 500 p-d. All of these structures are located in Las Sepulturas. The final cluster includes the remaining thirteen structures, most of which are located in the outlying rural areas. The energy in these structures is less than 100 p-d.

In a previous discussion of architectural energetics and the sociopolitical hierarchy at Copan (Abrams 1989:72), I suggested that minimally three clusters with possible subdivisions were evident, based solely on visual inspection of the bar chart of residential costs (Figure 16). The above analysis indicates, however, that six distinct levels of social power are a more appropriate estimate for Late Classic Copan society.

This hierarchy of energy costs in residences is consistent with the general lineage model of sociopolitical organization typifying the early state. The energy in Structure 10L-22 is clearly distinct from all others in the sample, reflecting considerably more power than any other single political position at

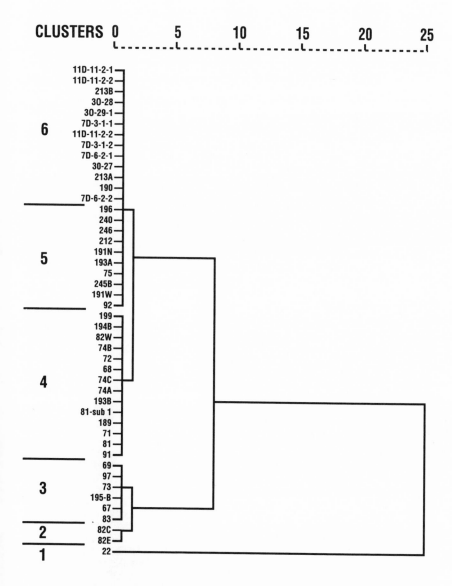

Figure 15. Cluster analysis of cumulative costs of residences.
Cluster 1: $N = 1$, mean $= 24,705$ p-d; Cluster 2: $N = 2$, mean $= 9,089$ p-d;
Cluster 3: $N = 6$, mean $= 4,466$ p-d; Cluster 4: $N = 14$, mean $= 1,878$ p-d;
Cluster 5: $N = 10$, mean $= 228$ p-d; Cluster 6: $N = 13$, mean $= 47$ p-d.

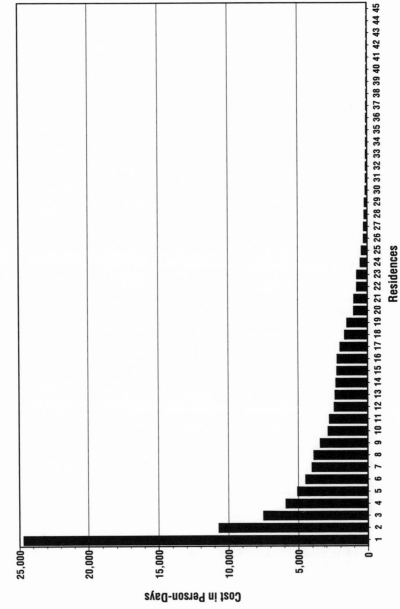

Figure 16. Cumulative costs of all residences

Copan. Structure 9N-82 reflected a second tier of power, consistent with the head of a very high-ranking maximal lineage unit (Sanders 1989:102). Within these lineage units are various hierarchic positions—ranked subdivisions within the corporate group, such as head of the minimal lineage, head of the minor lineage, and so forth. Based on the spatial distribution of these positions, heads of these lineage subdivisions were located in compounds of varying size; thus, while Structure 9N-82 might have housed the maximal lineage head, Structure 9N-69 may have housed the head of the next-highest-ranking lineage division, say, the administrator of the nested major lineage.

Thus far, four clusters of energy, interpreted as representing a royal elite and three ranked positions of subroyal elite (and their respective courtier), have been suggested. Beneath these various lineage administrative positions were statuses residing in the urban zone and ranking above that of commoner (the sixth cluster). This indicates that a complex composition of social statuses was represented within elite courtyards. The wide range of statuses within large compounds, for example, suggests that households of both high and low social power shared these residential spaces, a pattern perhaps reflecting the presence of relatives, domestics, cooks, and other relatively low-status individuals as coresidents of lineage administrators (Haviland 1981; Sanders 1981, 1989). If so, then the status of these retainers, based again on the energy expended in housing in these larger compounds, was higher than that of retainers for lower-ranking lineage administrators, and higher (to varying degrees) than the status of a "typical" commoner.

The final cluster represents the commoner status. In a few cases, the status of households within elite courtyards may not have differed greatly from that of the commoner. Structure 9M-190, for example, clearly falls within this lowest status; thus, there is some overlap between the residential expenditure and the etic status of commoner and that of occupants of low-ranking elite courtyards.

The spatial distribution of residences within these clusters reveals additional aspects of the lineage model as an expression of the segmentary state. Structure 10L-22 is located in the Main Center, at the heart of the Copan polity. The second cluster is completely embodied in Structure 9N-82, the House of the Bacabs (Webster 1989). The third cluster of social power is more dispersed. The five such structures in Group 9N-8 are found in four of the separate courtyards, suggesting that this intermediate level of social-spatial power was held by one or two members of these smaller social units. The sixth structure within this third cluster of social power is located in a dominant spatial position in Group 9M-22A, suggesting that the position of highest status within this compound was equivalent to that within smaller courtyards in Group 9N-8 such as B, C, and E, a conclusion consistent with Sheehy (1991). The distribution of residences within the fourth cluster spans Groups 9N-8, 9M-22A, and 9M-22B, suggesting that these representations of social power were roughly equivalent, despite their location within lineages of perhaps varying rank. Smaller courtyards, such as F within the very large Group 9N-8, were headed by a household equivalent in status to three households in Group 9M-22A, and one household—the head household—in Group 9M-22B. In addition, one structure in this fourth cluster, 9M-212, was classified within a Type 1 compound, 9M-24, in Las Sepulturas. The fact that this structure falls within this cluster confirms Gonlin's (1985) conclusion that some Type 1 structures in Las Sepulturas were occupied by households of higher status and power than those occupying Type 1 structures in the more rural sections of the Copan pocket. It should again be emphasized that some residences that absorbed rather modest amounts of energy, such as Structure 9N-75 (at 266 p-d), are located in larger residential compounds (in this case, Group 9N-8). Again, the commoner status is almost exclusively located in the nonurban zones.

This cluster analysis was conducted independent of the Willey-Leventhal typology, but, not surprisingly, it directly confirms that five-scheme hierarchy. To measure that correspondence, a Pearson's Correlation Coefficient analysis was conducted. The correspondence between the energy clusters and those generated by type was 0.6994, a significant correlation but not an extremely high one (say, in the 0.90 range). This again confirms that a wide range of power and status was spatially clustered in single courtyards or compounds, especially in the higher-status Type 3 and Type 4 compounds. In effect, the present analysis refines the measurement of social power that structured the Willey-Leventhal typology. This spatial clustering yields a continuum of costs for Types 1–4 and thus statuses (Figures 17–20).

Scrutiny of the sixth cluster suggests that there were no real *power* differentials within the commoner segment of Maya society, although there were undoubtedly *status* distinctions based on age and wisdom as well as variations in energy based simply on fluctuations in the domestic cycle. As discussed above, the energetic differences within this inferred social category might best be explained as the result of variations in factors other than social and political power; in the case of urban-rural comparisons, the possible lack of contemporaneity must be considered (Webster and Freter 1990b).

In addition, this analysis, based solely on architectural energetics, indicates that there is no clustering of energy in residences below that of the

Cost of Type 1 Residences

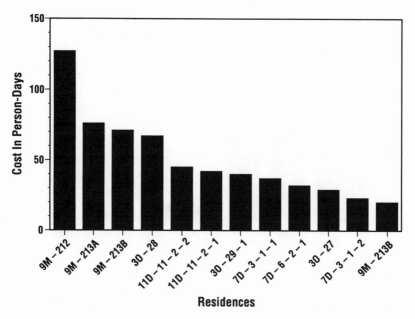

Figure 17. Cumulative costs of Type 1 residences

Cost of Type 2 Residences

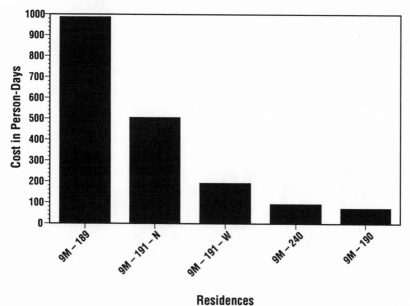

Figure 18. Cumulative costs of Type 2 residences

Cost of Type 3 Residences

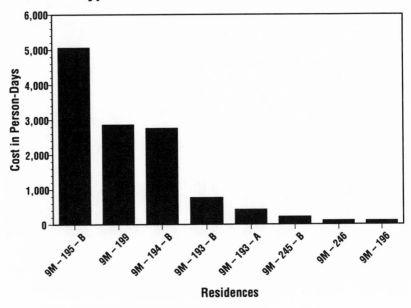

Figure 19. Cumulative costs of Type 3 residences

Cost of Type 4 Residences

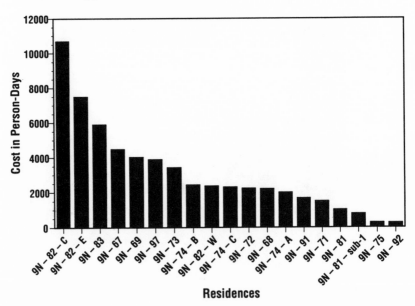

Figure 20. Cumulative costs of Type 4 residences

commoner status, and thus no instituted underclass. A permanent "slave" status does not appear to have existed at Late Classic Copan. Further studies of alternative databases, especially at sites containing perishable and platformless structures, should address this important question.

The analysis of the energetic costs of residences allows us to define, using the terminology of the lineage model detailed above, the general structure of sociopolitical relations during the Late Classic period (see Table 11 for calculations). Households of commoners, as well as those of relatively low-status retainers and domestics (Clusters 5 and 6), are represented by 85 percent of all residences at Late Classic Copan. The remaining 15 percent are classified as "elite" residences; this category includes the households of powerful royalty as well as high-status retainers and advisers of the elite. Within this broad category of the "elite," 10 percent fall within the lower to medium range of social power (Cluster 4), representing elites of intermediate rank. The final 5 percent of houses were occupied by the highest-ranking families at Copan, with less than 1 percent of these representing the household of the king. This general proportion of commoners to elites is consistent with that estimated for Tikal (Haviland 1985) and Dzibilchaltun (Kurjack 1974) and corroborates the findings of Webster (1992) at Copan.

This pyramid of architectural energetic costs confirms the general segmentary or lineage model for the Late Classic Maya state at Copan, characterized by hierarchic and nested social corporate units headed by a ruling elite. The commoners represented the most populous segment within society, with commoner households articulated in relatively egalitarian relationships. Lineage administrators, who served some proportion of households within the broader social network, represented a more ranked set of status and power relationships, topped by the maximal lineage head and his court. Finally, the highest-ranking lineage represented the state, headed by the king of Copan. Those individuals within the upper-elite ranks of the lineage and the state represented a stratified segment of society, despite their social affiliation within a ranked lineage organization. This conceptualization of stratification assumes a horizontal and restricted sphere of exchange and interaction involving only those lineage elite such that they share more in common with each other than with lower-ranked individuals within the lineage that they head. In essence, these elite members form a distinct political special-interest group. In addition, within the social hierarchy, there was no discernible underclass beneath the status of commoner. This does not mean there were no historic cases of slaves, immigrants, or other disenfranchised individuals who may have held a lower status. Rather, it suggests that a perma-

Table 11. Hierarchic Social Structure Based on Residential Cost

1. Two Lower Social Categories (residences of less than 500 p-d)
   Percentage of these residences by type:

	In Urban Zones	In Nonurban Zones
Single	100%	100%
Type 1	100%	100%
Type 2	60%	100%
Type 3	50%	80%
Type 4	0%	20%

2. Urban Core (Main Center, El Bosque, and Las Sepulturas)
   Estimated number of total residences = 853

	Total Residences by Type	Residences in Lower Categories
Single	15	15
Type 1	166	166
Type 2	265	159
Type 3	125	63
Type 4	256	0
Type 5	26	0
	853	403

3. Rural Copan Pocket
   Estimated total residences = 1,729

	Total Residences by Type	Residences in Lower Categories
Single	183	183
Type 1	978	978
Type 2	403	403
Type 3	126	101
Type 4	39	8
	1,729	1,673

4. Rural Zone
   Estimated total residences = 778

	Residences by Type	Residences in Lower Categories
Single	127	127
Type 1	519	519
Type 2	120	120
Type 3	12	10
	778	776

Table 11. (*continued*)

5. Total percentage of Copaneco households designated as houses of commoners or retainers of the elite: 2,852/3,360 = 85%

6. Percentage of households categorized as elite, including the courtier of the elite = 15%
    Of these, percentage of households in Cluster 4 (lower-ranked elite) = 67%, or 10% of all households at Copan.
    Of these, percentage of households in Clusters 1, 2 and 3 = 33%, or 5% of all households at Copan.

Note: Settlement and demographic data are drawn from Webster and Freter 1990b.

nent lower class was not part of the hierarchy of social power at Late Classic Copan. Interestingly, this lack of an underclass confirms to some degree the overarching assessment of the Classic Maya as representing an early state since more expansionary empires tend to produce substandard housing as a correlate to their greater social complexity (Abrams 1989:60).

Stratification and the Role of Architecture

Thus far, I have presented architecture as a valuable artifact in reflecting social power relations. Again, this use of architecture as a signature of social power within the state is simply an application of Childe's (1950) observation that the state as a political system contains the varied means (including force or threat of force) to ensure compliance by the populace (i.e., labor force) in state projects. More than simply an analytic means through which social relations are reconstructed, architecture and construction have also been considered active—i.e., playing a causative role—in the formation and maintenance of these power and status relationships.

Most of the statements or models connecting architecture with the process of state formation and growth involve the often-articulated concepts of social solidarity and power legitimization, both of which are considered by many as being embodied in the form of public architecture. It should be noted that public architecture is typically and correctly assumed to include temples and shrines as well as some civic constructions such as ball courts and public plazas. It could certainly be argued, however, that residential structures of the nobility, including the upper-lineage elite and the ruling-state elite, were also conceived of by the Maya as being to some degree "public," thus blurring this dichotomy.

The concept of social solidarity has long been a part of social science, its roots reaching back to Durkheim. The basic principle is that a human society, in order to effectively function as a more adaptive (i.e., energetically effective) unit, must create mechanisms that foster and maintain cooperative sentiment among its members. For societies with relatively few members, these mechanisms are largely grounded in kinship. However, as human societies increase in size and expand in social differentiation and social inequality, additional mechanisms beyond those of kinship must be created to offset the increasing entropic tendency of the system to evolve into a less complex state—that is, to "collapse." In this context, one mechanism often cited to foster such cooperation is participation in public construction projects (McGuire and Schiffer 1983:281). Archaeologists have refined this concept by suggesting that those periods of greatest stress on the social system (e.g., the earlier stages of state formation and consolidation) should correlate with times of greatest public architectural activity (Webster 1976; Trigger 1990). In the case of the Maya, Schele and Miller (1986:105) support this idea by stating that Late Preclassic architecture served "vital social functions of tying disparate groups together into a coherent whole." Hammond (1977:74) also refers to the "friction-reducing effect" of architectural construction projects and observes that "the aggrandizement of the ceremonial center increases the stake each individual has in the system and focuses loyalty in a centripetal manner."

This concept of social cohesion fits in with the concept of political legitimization, with large-scale architecture serving to convince the population of the reality of power (Trigger 1990:122). This is absolutely consistent with materialist thought, which places art and architecture in the role of justifying, legitimizing, and reifying a structure of power that benefits the creators and controllers of those symbols. In a very interesting study, Loten (1990) takes this notion of the presentation of power one step further by suggesting that Structure B-4-2, a large civic building at Altun Ha, Belize, was not only built to visually reflect symbols of power but also to actually mimic a supernatural entity. Certainly Maya rulers and lineage elite were quite aware of their positions of power and were equally cognizant of the varied ideological means and strategies of ensuring their enviable positions within the sociopolitical hierarchy.

As noted in the description of improved masonry structures, these residences generally expressed rather limited variability in form. A large part of that continuity was a consequence of purely mechanical factors; there are just so many ways, for example, to build a stable vaulted roof. On the other hand, some part of that continuity may be understood in the context of legitimization. It is reasonable to suggest that symbols that have been successful in validating political power through a particular psychological connectivity (or, more simply, long-term familiarity) are less likely to change dramatically over time, or will change only after they have lost their effectiveness.

Major stages of growth in political power correlate with architectural growth at Copan. Based on the interpretation of glyphic data, it has been suggested that either the first or second ruler, named Yax-K'uk-Mo, assumed power in A.D. 435 (Fash and Stuart 1991). Regardless of whether this ruler is seen as a powerful chief or a king, the emergence of that position is coeval with significant construction. Architectural data from the Great Plaza (Cheek 1983, 1986) and the East Court (Sharer, Miller, and Traxler 1992) indicate that about A.D. 400 there was a relative burst in construction activity involving civic architecture. In addition, there appears to be at Copan a second major episode of growth in the period A.D. 600–700, coinciding with the reign of Smoke-Jaguar. This growth in civic construction (Cheek 1986; Sharer, Miller, and Traxler 1992) is concomitant with a sizable increase in population and intensification of settlement nucleation (Webster and Freter 1990a; Freter 1992; Webster, Sanders, and van Rossum 1992). Collectively, these data support the correlation between increases in political power differentials and elite-sponsored construction projects.

While I would argue that political legitimization played an equally influential role in the manipulation of architectural symbols within the context of elite strategies, social solidarity, if developed at all, perhaps existed more with lower-energy projects, as in A.D. 400, rather than the higher-energy projects of A.D. 700. We can speculate that the psychological mechanism underlying this pattern is that collective sentiment tends to erode with increasing demands by the state.

If either social solidarity or political legitimization is assumed to be the motivation for large architectural projects, then they must be recognized as functionalistic. However, from the perspective of selection, the above discussion is not a simplistic correlative and ex post facto argument; rather, it suggests an underlying evolutionary causality based on individual perceptions of maintaining or enhancing quality of life, whether it be a commoner benefiting in many ways through participation in construction activities or a member of the elite benefiting through the solidification of power positions. Furthermore, it does not address the question of the distribution of resources, but rather considers the social, economic, and political consequences of construction as they influence the overall effectiveness of harnessing greater amounts of energy relative to alternatives. Hypothetically, those rulers of emergent states who selected for modesty, eschewing architectural display, lowered their effectiveness to compete against rivals.

As a correlate to the conceptualization of architecture as a means of *legitimizing* power, more direct economic considerations have been suggested that view architecture as a means of *generating* power. Price (1984:226–227) has suggested that, as state institutions emerged from those institutions characteristic of ranked society, the critical factor of production that provided political leverage among competing chiefs was labor rather than land. Given relatively low population densities, increased access to greater amounts of labor by any single chief was the key to producing surplus food energy in the competition among chiefs. In essence, ranked societies were forced to underuse land due to this limited supply of labor and thus did not reach the full potential of agricultural productivity within a particular mode of production. Price recognizes public or monumental construction as an etic signature of the ability of a chief to produce and consume surplus energy, thus serving as a conspicuous display of resources and power, regardless of motivation. According to Price, public architecture served to attract labor from smaller chiefdoms or other political units, those individuals presumably hoping to increase their quality of life by attaching themselves to a polity controlling greater amounts of resources, resources that the polity could afford to "waste" in architecture. This argument is echoed by Demarest (1991), who considers public architecture less a symbol of power than an artifact that can generate power through its capacity to manipulate political and economic support. Demarest argues that Maya rulers, lacking firm political control of economic resources, created symbols in the form of elaborate architecture as "theater," analogous to kingdoms in Southeast Asia.

We must be cautious, however, when considering architecture as a generator of power. Architecture itself serves at best as a proximate cause of power in its role as an attractor of labor. In the absence of other factors requisite for generating energy, such as land and water, the architecture itself does not generate energy per se and should not be equated with ultimate causality (Price 1984; Trigger 1990). In essence, this consideration of architecture as a generator of power need not be conceived of as an "either-or" question; rather, architecture should be evaluated in terms of its effectiveness as an attractor of labor, with that labor differential in the context of agricultural productivity then serving as the measure of value effected through architecture.

This very important focus on the role of architecture in attracting labor, particularly in the context of state formation, deserves further consideration. Whereas most attention is directed at monumental public buildings, perhaps as much analytic value lies in a consideration of the "attractive" quality of improved residential structures. The residences of chiefs are, almost as an ethnologic fact, clearly above the standard quality of housing; presumably the residences of the first kings were similarly of higher quality. Thus, elite residential architecture may have also served as a symbolic attractor of labor, as did elite public architecture.

Improved housing, however, is more than symbolic of power; improved housing confers to its occupants a direct increase in the biopsychological quality of life, as was established in Chapter 3. Improved residential forms were not restricted to only the ruling elite; in fact, with the formation and growth of the state, the overall quality of housing hypothetically increased for society as a whole. Specifically, greater numbers of individuals were included within the ranks of the lineage administration and greater numbers of commoners resided within elite courtyards, the latter confirmed by the wide range of energy costs in these large compounds. Further, it is likely that most core members of the early state benefited from the instituting of state relations. In contradistinction to Marxist notions of exploitation, I would argue that the early state *perhaps necessarily* provided an overall improved quality of life for the core population, expressed in some cases in housing. Certainly the improvements were not equally shared or uniformly distributed among all households. Nonetheless, greater energy harnessed by the early state was likely redistributed in part to many households, with some of that energy being expended in housing. This proposed access to better housing within the early state may have been facilitated through access to a greater network of labor, through the elimination of some egalitarian ideological sanctions that precluded greater energy expenditures in housing, and through periodic access to specialists. Similarly, access to improved housing may have been part of the reward system among state and lineage elite, providing incentives for ranked administrators to fully participate in promoting the interests of the state.

This discussion has again returned us to housing and the notion that differential access to housing plays an active role in decision making. The organizational structure through which these various houses were built is the topic of the next chapter.

7

The Organization
of Construction Labor

The hierarchic structure of sociopolitical power at Late Classic Copan was created and maintained through the differential access to basic and necessary resources, one of which was human labor. In this chapter I will continue the discussion and analysis of social power by considering one expression of that power revealed by architectural energetics—the specific organizational forms of labor used in the construction process. The value of using architectural energetics in such an analysis is twofold. First, residential architecture cuts across all social levels and, barring inappropriate sampling, should then reflect the full range of organization and concomitant differential access to labor throughout society. Second, architecture is sufficiently costly as to make increasingly large demands of labor prohibitive to some individuals or segments within society; as such, the selection of distinct systems of labor access by social units can be analyzed within an evolutionary framework (Price 1982).

The ability to discern labor systems illustrates a case in point of the methodological and analytic value of estimating specific person-day costs rather than a more general volumetric assessment of architecture. Unlike the analysis of social power presented in Chapter 6, which was based on the cumulative cost of construction, the reconstruction of labor systems is based on the cost of construction minus reuse, since the best approximations of energy expended during actual episodes of construction appear to be the most appropriate energetic units of analysis.

Models of Labor Organization

The first step in reconstructing the various labor systems at Late Classic Copan involves a presentation of descriptive models concerning the organization of labor, and such a springboard has been provided by Stanley Udy in
The Organization of Work (1959). Through a statistical analysis of several elemental work activities, including construction, Udy was able to isolate and
describe basic principles of labor organization and demonstrate a positive
correlation between cultural complexity, energy, and scale of construction.
With minor modifications, Udy defines complexity in the organization of
construction labor as an expression of the interaction of three primary variables: (1) the system of recruitment that designates specific categories of
membership (principally, kin or nonkin) and concomitant social ramifications of such recruitment; (2) the system of rewards for participation in construction projects (principally, balanced or imbalanced exchange); and (3) the
degree of task differentiation, involving both horizontal differentiation (i.e.,
specialists without significant status elevation) and vertical differentiation
(i.e., managers, administrators, and high-status specialists). The linking of
increasing behavioral and institutional complexity with energy aligns Udy's
work with similar anthropological studies concerned with better understanding the continuum of systemic complexity within an evolutionary perspective (e.g., Chapple and Coon 1942; McGuire 1983). By considering these
three criteria, Udy is able to generate two very broad categories of labor
organization—familial recruitment and custodial recruitment. The essential
distinction between these two broad categories is that familial recruitment
involves exchange between approximate social equals, whereas custodial recruitment involves unbalanced exchange between social positions of unequal
power. Familial recruitment is further divided into three subcategories, and
custodial recruitment, into two. What follows is a description of these five
systems of labor organization.

Familial Recruitment

Familial Reciprocal. Recruitment within the familial reciprocal organization
is based on membership within an ascribed kin group: "Personnel are drawn
from some kind of kinship group, which may range in size from a nuclear
family to a ramified set of extended kin relations" (Udy 1959:56). In this
system, the use of labor may or may not be expected in return, following the
divisions of generalized and balanced reciprocity. The former is characterized
by "transactions that are putatively altruistic, transactions on the line of

assistance given and, if possible and necessary, assistance returned" (Sahlins 1972:193). In the latter, exchange of labor is such that "the reciprocation is the customary equivalent to the thing received and is without delay" (ibid.: 194). In terms of equivalence and immediacy of return, in reality there is a continuum between these two types of reciprocity, and the exchange of labor for construction should be conceived of as part of a broader constellation of reciprocal relations.

Udy illustrates the familial reciprocal system with the case of labor exchange in the Philippines (1959:77). He describes the *bolhon* system, wherein a small group of neighbors exchange equal amounts of labor on a rotational basis, with obligations thus discharged upon completion of the rotation. This reciprocal system is typically associated with agriculture since the quantity of labor needed and the timing are relatively fixed features of the work schedule. The *palihog* system is more typical of construction, wherein neighbors are simply asked to contribute labor with an understanding that relatively equal amounts of labor will be reciprocated upon request.

The specific scale of the familial reciprocal system—from a son helping with roof repair to a handful of neighbors helping with complete house construction—is limited by the number of laborers one can or wishes to tap; if too many individuals are requested, the obligatory return of labor may be too great a responsibility to accept. In my opinion, this general category could be subdivided based on kin distance and other variables. Nonetheless, for the archaeological case at hand, this one broad category will suffice.

Familial Contractual. The second typological designation of organizational complexity of labor is what Udy terms familial contractual, wherein "auxiliary workers are added to the familial structure by virtue of a contractual agreement between them and the family proprietor. It is agreed that they will aid the family in certain work for a certain time, and, generally, for specific compensation" (Udy 1959:73). This is essentially the familial reciprocal system with appended specialists. Ethnographic accounts of this system have been described with reference to the housebuilder-carpenter guilds of Oceania (Goldman 1970; Gifford 1929; Handy et al. 1924), although in this system a specialist "only rarely . . . builds a house for a commoner, and only when the commoner is so fortunate as to possess something suitable as a present" (Gifford 1929:146). Archaeologically, it may be impossible to distinguish this system from the more generalized familial reciprocity; even the recovery of spatially discrete but limited construction tool kits may be insufficient to test for the presence of contracted specialists.

Community Contractual. The community contractual category of labor system—Udy's agency form of a familial contractual system—subsumes those cases in the anthropological literature wherein architecture is built through the use of an established community work party. It differs from the familial reciprocal system in that larger numbers of people of varying degrees of kin distance are involved, with a concomitant increase in internal organizational complexity. One ethnographic account of large work parties assisting families in house construction is described among the Dahomey (Herskovits 1938:64). All members of this work party, or *dokpwe,* are compensated in what is essentially a balanced reciprocal system; however, the managers of the *dokpwe,* including the hereditary head, the foreman, the record-keeper, and the spokesperson, all receive additional compensation for services rendered. In addition, participation in the *dokpwe* is often inconvenient for some, so an individual has the prerogative to pay members of the *dokpwe* in order to avoid having to participate. Thus we see emergent elements of separation from the reciprocal obligations expressed by those persons with adequate resources (cf. Bennett 1968). A similar communal organization, called the *fagina,* has been described for the contemporary Maya (Redfield and Villa R. 1964).

Custodial Recruitment

In societies where differences in power and status are evident through differential economic access, there is necessarily some set of unbalanced exchanges and restricted spheres of exchange involving unequal statuses (Fried 1967). In terms of construction, one primary mechanism for creating an unbalanced exchange between households is the substitution of some other good for that of labor. This substitution makes accountability more difficult and manipulation of the exchange more possible. This type of exchange, characterized as negative reciprocity (Sahlins 1972:195), correlates with, and in part perhaps contributes to, social power differentials. Udy (1959:78) terms this general category of labor organization custodial recruitment, which consists of two subcategories: festive custodial and corvée.

Festive Custodial. The most balanced form of custodial recruitment is what I will term festive custodial, equivalent to Erasmus' festive reciprocal system (1956:445). In this system, labor is given to a socially more powerful individual in return for a feast or party upon completion of the project. The recipient of this labor generally does not offer his labor in return and does not contribute labor during the project, which is the critical distinction between this system and all forms of the familial recruitment system. Various cases of this type of labor organization system can be found in the ethnographic literature (e.g., Gifford 1929; Hiroa 1934).

The festive custodial system seems to be just that—festive. As with the *dokpwe,* some participants in a festive custodial system of labor do not work very hard and some simply "participate" by encouraging others to work. It is an expression of social exchange wherein the social differential between the receiver and giver of labor is implicit and often consciously made inconspicuous. In more benign expressions of this system (e.g., among societies with limited ranking), there may be no unbalancing of exchange value, making the distinction between this system and the community contractual system rather enigmatic. Erasmus (1956:448), in describing this type of labor system, notes that, although the host does not return labor to most of the participants, the host often *must* return labor to close relatives, thus revealing its transitional nature and suggesting the variable expressions of this system. Archaeologically, this system may be difficult to distinguish from larger reciprocal systems; perhaps the status of the host (as reflected in architectural costs or other comparative measures) may provide the best means for inferring which form of labor access and organization was likely used.

The potential for increasing the imbalances of exchange are inherent in this festive custodial system. Erasmus (ibid.:448), for example, noted that "in hacienda or 'feudal' situations where land owners control their labor through the ability to withhold perquisites, such as the use of subsistence plots, pasture land, firewood, and roads, attendance at 'festive' work parties becomes almost mandatory and the composition of the work groups may be quite fixed." This more extreme form of a festive custodial system may be instituted by (1) excluding close relatives from the labor pool and thus eliminating any social requisite for return labor and (2) increasing the absolute amount of labor expected from individuals who are becoming more economically disenfranchised from resources controlled by the socially more powerful host of such festive work parties.

Corvée. Once the imbalance between host and participant becomes marked and the giving of labor is de facto obligatory (i.e., a tax), a threshold has been crossed and the system may be considered corvée labor. The very definition of corvée as a labor system involves an instituted imbalance; under European feudal law, corvée was unpaid labor from a vassal to a lord for a day or longer (Webster's New International Dictionary 1942). Thus, a corvée system emerges from a festive custodial system as the degree of instituted imbalance of exchange is increased.

Like all other systems described here, the corvée system varies considerably. In general, relatively large numbers of participants are expected to contribute labor with no expectation of direct return. In one ethnographic description of a rather "low-energy" corvée system, Henry (1928:138) states that, after King Pomare I subjugated all of Tahiti and Mo'orea, a new *marae* was built "of splendid dimensions. . . . It was the combined work of all Tahiti and Mo'orea . . . and every able-bodied man of the realm furnished a stone from land or sea for its construction." In more powerful state systems, laborers are obliged to provide far more than "a stone," and the scale of imbalance is often intentionally severe, with participants having no option but to contribute to large-scale construction projects initiated and managed by the state. During the Han Dynasty (206 B.C.–A.D. 220), for example, every male between the ages of twenty-two (or twenty-three) and fifty-six supplied one month per year of labor to the state. This labor was in addition to two years of obligatory military service (Loewe 1968:75). Given this scale of corvée, the amount of labor available was staggering. In 109 B.C., tens of thousands of conscripts toiled in the construction of dikes to control the flooding of the Yellow River (ibid.:73). Using convict labor as well as farmer-conscripts, the Chinese state, in A.D. 63, used 2,690 laborers on road construction projects that totaled approximately 770,000 p-d (ibid.:72). Zhongshu (1983:2) noted that just one wall surrounding the Han capital city of Changan required approximately 145,000 laborers for an estimated thirty days, or over four million person-days. I imagine that one way of becoming "convict labor" was to refuse to be "farmer labor"; in cases such as these, the "return" for participation may have been avoidance of imprisonment. Certainly, the most severe forms of corvée are highly susceptible to the worst abuses of unbalanced reciprocity.

Energy Requirements and Labor Organization

The presentation above outlines various idealized forms of labor organization for construction. These systems, however, are generalizations, and, as stated earlier, considerable behavioral variation exists within any specific system. For example, European feudal lords, the overseers of corvée labor, occasionally found themselves and their immediate family members performing physical labor on construction projects in order to meet completion deadlines set by a higher-ranking lord or king. Certainly specific historic cases of lords and serfs working together in no way negated or obfuscated the fact that relations of social power and concomitant obligations continued to exist between these two very different social classes.

These various systems correlate in general with energy expenditure and thus can be viewed from a materialist-selectionist perspective. The familial reciprocal system is based on limited economic-energetic access, which is equally low among kin or other peers. There are few if any viable options to accessing labor except that of establishing a balanced exchange involving social equals. Long-term leadership positions are thus minimized, the project scale is limited, and few if any specialists are required, all predicated by the low energy expenditure. As differential access emerges, some individuals are able to avoid the labor obligation system (Erasmus 1956; Bennett 1968), just as some Dahomeans will buy their way out of the *dokpwe*. Once this differential access is instituted, consumable surplus becomes available and larger projects commissioned by the wealthier segment of society are possible. These higher-energy projects invariably require more laborers, more specialists, and concomitantly more hierarchic positions of management. Since these more complex systems only correspond with higher levels of social power, they are additive in nature; that is, they will coexist with low-energy systems, such as the familial and community reciprocal systems.

Ideally, I would like to further support the general ethnological link between labor systems and energy with a wide range of specific structures and their costs, drawn from the ethnographic record. However, this can only partially be achieved. Table 12 provides a sample of ethnographic cases that link the amount of energy expended in construction projects with the various subcategories of familial recruitment. As one would expect, there is a clear association between very low expenditures of energy in construction and the familial system. Conversely, data from very powerful state systems (cited above) link extremely high expenditures of energy with the corvée system. Clearly, however, gaps exists in the ethnographic record, principally concerning the energy expended in those more intermediate systems. There is, nonetheless, adequate empirical support from the ethnographic literature that connects increasing energy with increasing organizational complexity.

Late Classic Architecture, Energy, and Labor Systems

Perhaps the soundest way to reconstruct the unobservable labor systems of the Late Classic Maya at Copan is to begin with the least costly structures, since we have the clearest analogs for those buildings. It is a reasonable inference that all basic wattle and daub residences located outside the urban bar-

Table 12. Energy Requirements and Familial Recruitment Systems

Energy (p-d)	Group	System[a]	Source
0.5	Eskimo	FR	Boas 1964
2	San	I	Lee 1979
2–3	Siriono	I/FR	Holmberg 1969
25	Costa Rica (peasant)	FR	Lange and Ryberg 1972
28	Tikopia	FR	Firth 1965
24–160	Copan	FR	Abrams this volume
65	Kekchi	FR	Wilk and Rathje 1982
86	Chan Kom	CR	Redfield and Villa R. 1964
100	Kaoka	FR/FCON	Hogbin 1914
131	Bantu	FR	Knuffel 1973
132	Zinacantan	FR	Vogt 1969

[a]Familial recruitment systems: I = individual effort; FR = familial reciprocity; FCON = familial contractual; CR = community reciprocity

rios and costing less than approximately 100 p-d were constructed within a familial reciprocal labor system. If a residential structure required 100 p-d and was built in twenty days during the agricultural off-season, then only five laborers were required. We know that residential construction today in the Copan Valley is conducted during the dry agricultural off-season for a variety of ecological and economic reasons, and the construction of a wattle and daub house over a period of twenty or thirty days is quite reasonable (Abrams 1984a). Thus, commoner households needing repair or new construction would have tapped labor from within their own courtyard or from courtyards containing close kin or friends, with the expectation that labor would be returned to the participants in future construction projects. As stated in the previous chapter, we currently do not know very much about the spatial dimension of kinship, and thus it may be more appropriate to conceive of the pool of reciprocal labor as being drawn from a network of relatives and friends that might include any number of courtyards.

Several structures in the sample demanded rather low energy, yet they are spatially associated with elite courtyards in Las Sepulturas. For example, the energy expended in the construction of Structures 9M-245B, 9M-246, and 9M-196, three residences within Group 9M-22A, was 214 p-d, 105 p-d, and 101 p-d, respectively (see Figure 13 and Appendix A). In the previous analysis of general sociopolitical structure, these residences were assigned to households of modest status, representing the homes of domestics or economic retainers serving minor lineage administrators. These structures clearly fall within the range of architecture that could have been built within the same familial reciprocal system as the rural basic structures were. Thus a nonelite household residing within an elite courtyard could simply tap relatives, as might any other commoner. However, the association of these structures with higher-energy structures suggests that other variables may be considered beyond that of energy. It is equally possible that some modest form of a festive custodial system, drawing the few laborers necessary from courtyards of low-status individuals (residing within the urban or rural zones), was responsible for construction of these houses, based on the high status and power of the subroyal administrator coresiding in that courtyard. In the case at hand, the high power of the individual residing within Structure 9M-195B, an important lineage administrator, may have been extended to draw labor from lineage-affiliated commoners in the construction of the home of his low-ranking clients.

The houses of the elite within Las Sepulturas, the costs of which ranged from roughly 1,000 p-d to 11,000 p-d, were likely constructed within some variant of the festive custodial system or, for the costliest structures, a low-level corvée system. Structure 9M-189 (Figure 13), for example, required 986 p-d for construction; if built over a sixty-day period, then seventeen laborers were required. These individuals were almost certainly drawn in part from lower-ranking courtyards since it is doubtful that seventeen able-bodied individuals, susceptible to conscription for heavy construction labor, resided within that courtyard. In fact, recent work by Diamanti (1991:232) indicates that Group 9M-22B housed only between sixteen and twenty people; thus the labor for constructing Structure 9M-189 must have been drawn from other courtyards. Surrounded by residential courtyards occupied by high-status households, it is probable that labor was drawn from nonurban, commoner courtyards.

Construction of Structure 9M-195-B, in Group 9M-22A, required 5,058 p-d (Figure 13). In broad terms, if the structure was built in sixty days, then eighty-four persons were required; if built during a span of one hundred days, then fifty-one were needed. Again, labor from outside this courtyard must have been conscripted. According to Diamanti (ibid.), forty-four to fifty-five people resided within this group, again representing insufficient labor for construction. Certainly several lower-ranking courtyards must have been tapped for labor. Either a large festive custodial system, or perhaps even a low-level corvée system, was likely in effect. The occupant of this struc-ture—a high-ranking administrator within the lineage—had sufficiently great social power as to preclude any direct return of labor; at best, some return in the form of food was perhaps provided upon completion of the project. As further support for the likelihood of a custodial system, de Landa noted that "the common people built at their own expense the houses of the lords" (Tozzer 1941:86).

The energy demanded in the final construction of Structure 9N-82-C—8,567 p-d—is the greatest cost thus far determined for any *single* construction episode within Las Sepulturas (Figure 12). The number of conscripts ranged from perhaps 100 to 130, and it is likely that a modest form of corvée system, with labor now considered a tax, provided the instituted context for this architectural project. This number of laborers would have been conscripted from perhaps ten to fifteen courtyards. Although it is certainly possible that a festive custodial system was responsible, I believe that some form of corvée was in effect based on the very high relative and absolute cost of the structure and the very high social power of the occupant, just below that of the ruler of Copan.

Either system—festive custodial or low-level corvée—would have been available to maximal lineage heads and could have involved the return of food during or after the construction process. Although perhaps impossible to test, a structure located between Group 9N-8A and 9N-8H—Structure 9N-78—has been identified as a kitchen (Widmer 1993). Unattached to any extant courtyard, this structure may have served as a food-processing locus during communal affairs of various types, and perhaps one such occasion would have been lineage-sponsored construction projects. Obsidian hydra-tion dates from this structure indicate contemporaneity with Patios H and A (AnnCorinne Freter, personal communication, 1992). If accepted, this evi-dence would strengthen the suggestion that a relatively modest form of cor-vée, if even that, was operative.

One very important aspect of this energetic analysis is that the general number of participants may be estimated. As stated above, between 80 and 130 laborers were likely conscripted in the construction of Structure 9N-82C, a maximal estimate assuming construction within one dry season. This and similar analyses reveal that lineage administrators did not, or perhaps could not, draft labor from beyond their political jurisdiction. In a segmen-tary state, hierarchic elite positions would have concomitant numbers of households from which to draw labor. Nonetheless, it appears that lineage elite were restricted in their labor pool to those affiliated with that particular lineage; thus, even the most powerful lineage elite administrator could not cut across lineage lines.

The palatial residence in the sample—Structure 10L-22—required the energetic equivalent of 24,705 p-d (Figure 11). Regardless of how one wishes to divide that figure into specialists and nonspecialists, construction certainly involved a few hundred common laborers (Abrams 1987). As an exercise, I have calculated that over 300 individuals participated in its construction. This labor estimate strongly points to a system of corvée, with personnel conscripted from several maximal lineage units. This indicates that, as a general statement, the rulers of Copan during the Late Classic period were considerably more powerful than any single lineage head in their capacity to access labor.

The scale of corvée available to and maintained by the Late Classic rulers of Copan deserves discussion since the interpretation of political power involving these Maya rulers can be further assessed. I have suggested elsewhere (Abrams 1987) that, despite the establishment of a corvée, the numbers of laborers as well as the number of times any individual was conscripted in royal architectural projects was still relatively low compared with other state systems. This assessment may be refined or even rejected once additional data and analysis from the Main Group are available. However, at present I am assuming that the construction of Structure 10L-22 by the state represented the annual output by the state corvée system. If, then, roughly 300 conscripts were required in the construction of Structure 10L-22 (the cost of which assumed no reuse), and roughly 25,000 people lived within the domain of the Late Classic Copan rulers (of which 20 percent were susceptible to conscription as household heads), then any adult male would be obliged to work on the state-sponsored corvée projects once every fifteen or twenty years. This might then require each individual to work for the state in this capacity about two or three times per lifetime. If segments of the population besides adult males were involved, then these figures drop even further. By comparison, the dynastic Chinese case cited above indicates that each individual was required to participate in state projects one month each year for over thirty years. The average Maya household head was required to provide maximally 180 days to the state (60 days × 3 events), whereas the average Chinese household head was required to provide 900 days to the state (30 days × 30 events), or five times the energetic contribution to the state per lifetime. From this comparative exercise it is reasonable to infer that some demographic, political, and economic limitations existed that restricted the scale of corvée in terms of the expressed degree of imbalance, and this measure of checks and balances may be endemic to the hierarchic lineage organization characteristic of the Maya and other early states.

One remaining question concerns when these various systems were instituted. Certainly the familial system for construction existed from the earliest Maya house. The creation of a civic center in ca. A.D. 400 may correspond with the emergence or expansion of a ranked society, in which case we may project the establishment of a festive custodial system. Only after the architectural energetics are calculated for this time period, however, will we be able to comparatively assess the scale of that recruitment system. The corvée, in its most extreme form of imbalance for the Maya, was likely instituted with the establishment of a position of king; of course, this establishment of the "state" was itself a dynamic process, with historic contests of power often distorting typologic purity (e.g., Sharer 1991). Based on the data concerning construction (Cheek 1983, 1986; Sharer, Miller, and Traxler 1992) and demographic growth (Webster and Freter 1990a; Fash and Sharer 1991; Freter 1992; Webster, Sanders, and van Rossum 1992), it is reasonable to infer that the corvée was first established during the period A.D. 600–700. More labor from all maximal lineages was involved in state construction, although, as suggested, certain checks and balances existed that limited in some ways the continued increases in demand and exploitation of labor.

Implications of the Labor System

In this chapter I have presented architectural energetic data coupled with models of labor organization that suggest a hierarchic structure to labor access during the Late Classic period at Copan. Commoners would have relied upon peers—perhaps close kin or courtyard coresidents—to aid in house construction, with the expectation of return labor when requested. Lower-ranking administrators within the proposed ranked sociopolitical corporate structure would have been able to tap labor from within their restricted sociopolitical jurisdiction within the context of a communal work force. Increasingly more powerful elite members of each lineage would have been able to conscript correspondingly larger amounts of labor from within that social corporate unit in the context of a continuum of festive work obligations and emergent corvée labor. Finally, the rulers of the Copan state would have been able to conscript labor from all denizens of Copan, thus cutting across all lineage affiliations in the context of corvée labor, albeit one inhibited by social and political constraints.

It is important to emphasize that there were very distinct forms of labor access, corresponding in general with distinct levels of social power, but these forms of labor organization often differed in scale rather than structure. Thus, while the organization of labor access for commoners was substantively distinct from that for the ruling elite, the organization of labor available to households within each broad social category was in reality a continuum of expressed power.

One of the implications of this proposed hierarchic structure of labor recruitment and obligations is that it may represent the structure of labor distribution and access in other domains of the Late Classic Maya state, particularly concerning labor access for agricultural production. It is likely that the structure of labor access for construction was similar to that for agriculture, the former representing a physical signature of the latter. Within the context of this proposed hierarchic structure, then, each commoner farming household would have been involved in reciprocal exchange with select households during peak seasonal demands on labor, such as the harvesting of staples from *milpas*. This is in fact rather common, recorded for the sixteenth-century Maya (Tozzer 1941:96) and exemplified ethnographically by the *palihog* system of rotating labor exchange noted above.

In addition, some or all of these commoner households would have been required periodically—again, perhaps on a rotating basis—to provide concomitant amounts of labor or its energy equivalent in food to those ranked elite administrators within their specific lineage as well as to the state. At this stage of research we have no framework for proposing the amount of labor conscripted for suprahousehold agriculture, nor do we have any firm model for the amount of produce returned to the participants or to society at large. Nonetheless, it is certain that either surplus from household *milpas* and gardens was taxed or that some labor recruitment system for the working of lineage and state lands was in effect, although these two approaches to generating surplus need not be mutually exclusive. If future research concerning agriculture confirms the latter, however, then the proposed hierarchic structure of labor access for architecture may represent the best working hypothesis for the reconstruction of labor for agriculture.

8

Architecture and Economics

A final set of inferences derived from the energetics of architecture involves the reconstruction of economic specialization. The question of reconstructing and analyzing the growing complexity in the division of labor as expressed in the emergence and expansion of economic specialists has long been a focus of anthropological inquiry (e.g., Chapple and Coon 1942). This focus on economic specialization as a process having enormous ramifications for society has received particular attention in the case of the southern lowland Maya state (Adams 1970; Becker 1973; Rice 1981; Abrams 1987; McAnany and Isaac 1989). Much of the current research centers on discerning the cultural conditions under which specialization develops, the scale of specialization, and the place of specialists within the broader socioeconomic structure. This chapter will consider the scale and structure of economic specialization from the perspective of construction.

Houses and their construction are an integral part of the economy, defined as those collective mechanisms of production and distribution that provision society with goods and services (Polanyi 1957). The principal function of the house, as elaborated upon in Chapter 3, is to provide protection and shelter from the external environment, not only for the human occupants, but in many cases for animals and artifacts (such as tools), which are themselves part of the "goods" within society. Certainly humans may be identified as the most valued of goods for a wide range of reasons, one being that they are a primary source of labor. In this sense, the process of constructing houses, as part of the production technology, is equivalent to the manufacture of other protective features, such as storage facilities. In addition, houses are often the loci of economic activity and in that sense are directly linked to the production process (Gregory and Altman 1989:196).

Methodologically, the quantification of the production (construction) process allows one to reconstruct the probable position of construction personnel within the socioeconomic sphere. As stated, the structure of economic specialization in terms of construction may have been paralleled by that for other technologies, despite the general and hypothetical nature of that correspondence. The organizational principle underlying this assertion is evolutionary in nature: the least costly yet comparatively effective organizational mode will probabilistically be selected for. Since the increased use of preexisting systems tends to cost less than the establishment of new or significantly modified systems, the existing systems should represent the institutional matrix for emergent economic activities. The previous analysis served as an example: the reconstruction of labor systems was best understood within the framework of an existing hierarchical structure of lineage and state. The ensuing economic analysis continues this logical extension of the role of the hierarchic sociopolitical organization.

Generalized Labor: The Basic Form

The vast majority of houses at Late Classic Copan, being low-energy, basic houses, were built within a labor exchange system characterized by balanced reciprocity. For this reciprocal labor system to be effective, knowledge of construction activities had to be accessible to all participants in the system and capable of being effectively and readily transmitted to younger participants. Wauchope (1938:140) recognized this fact when he stated, "It is not surprising that almost every Indian knows the smallest details of house construction. . . . He watches and helps in the construction of houses as a child; he plans and supervises personally the construction of at least one of his own; he assists in the building of many townsmen's houses." This description is fully confirmed by other ethnographers (e.g., Wisdom 1940:189) as well as through my own survey of households in Copan. Of course, not all individuals are equally talented or share the same capabilities, inclinations, and work habits. Coupled with the fluctuations in the developmental cycle of each household, which result in differential access to immediate labor, this "natural" variability in skills supports the inference that the *kin network,* including courtyard coresidents and extending beyond spatial-residential proximity, might be the more powerful unit of analysis or conceptualization concerning the reciprocal exchange of construction labor.

In a broader picture of economic activities, it is quite common to find a mixed economic strategy among rural peasants today. Viewed from a cross-cultural perspective, most peasants tend to learn a wide range of economic skills as a means of offsetting risks and insecurities endemic to their economic circumstances. This is certainly true in Copan today. I was constantly impressed by the wide range of fundamental skills possessed by our workers. That same type of generalized knowledge and skill is evident in many rural sections of the United States. Focusing on rural Appalachian populations, for example, Halperin (1990) offers the concept of "multiple livelihood strategies," which behaviorally refers to the many skills that one must possess on a continuous basis in order to survive within a very insecure economic environment. The social and psychological constructs of self-sufficiency and independence that often characterize rural agrarian society are seen as probable ideological correlates to this generalized economic strategy. It is a reasonable projection that those skills required of the Maya commoners for basic house construction were part of this generalized economic strategy.

The presence of a reciprocal labor exchange system on the commoner level required common knowledge of fundamental construction skills, and the necessary procuring, manufacturing, and engineering skills were almost certainly learned within the context of the household. One specific case from the ethnographic literature is exemplary: Wisdom (1940:295) observed that young Chorti boys, beginning at the age of six or seven, are initiated into housebuilding responsibilities by adults and that they have mastered sufficient housebuilding skills by the age of twelve or thirteen. In a comparative overview of systems of learning, Goody (1989:234) concluded that most learning of generalized economic knowledge occurs within the context of a Domestic Mode of Production (Sahlins 1972), with this knowledge being transmitted principally from same-sex parents or siblings. Certainly the household or household network is clearly the most effective means of transmitting such information and providing experience concerning basic house construction.

Generalized Labor: The Improved Form

The leitmotiv of this book is that the prominence of ancient architectural ruins often has a profound influence on our perceptions about these buildings and the society that built them. One such expression of this influence is that the scale and aesthetic quality of monumental architecture must have required profound skill and complex organization, thus masking the relative *simplicity* of architectural and engineering skills requisite for construction.

This assessment is based on several lines of reasoning. First, a review of Lawrence Roys' (1934) classic description of engineering skills of the Maya reveals a marked simplicity in required skills for the successful construction of masonry structures (also Kaplan 1963:402). Second, masonry structures exhibit a striking redundancy in form; this limited variation in the improved form is due to physical engineering requirements as well as the desire to replicate known symbols of authority (see Chapter 7). One ramification of this repetition in form was that engineering skills did not undergo tremendous fluctuation through time. Third, masonry structures were built from very few raw materials, which, except for plaster and paint, were produced through simple reduction processes. In addition, the lack of more complex materials—for example, metals—precluded a range of additional construction techniques, such as the clamping of masonry blocks. Finally, difficult subsurface construction components were extremely rare in Maya architecture. I am not suggesting, however, that these buildings were "easy" to construct or that anyone could have designed and orchestrated their construction. Nor am I suggesting that construction knowledge was obvious or innate. Nonetheless, the notion that these buildings were the product of thousands of unskilled laborers and a huge number of skilled specialists toiling under the direction of some guild or corps of professional architects is perhaps unrealistic.

The criteria for discerning whether a task was conducted by a generalized or specialized laborer have been made quite explicit in the archaeological literature (e.g., Costin 1991). In the present analysis, I define specialist activities in part on the basis of the technological study of artifacts and features, but I further define generalized and specialized production on the basis of (1) the degree of required skills (based on my observations of construction tasks), (2) the energetic value of the product, and (3) the ideological associations with that specific architectural component.

The overall simplicity and redundancy involved in procurement and transport suggest that these operations were conducted by generalized laborers. All of the tasks in these operations involved heavy but not highly skilled labor. Quarrying stone, for example, is actually an amazingly straightforward task that requires very little training and skill. Similarly, the transport of materials required only a strong back and some sense of balance. For improved structures, the mean percentage of labor expended in performing these two operations was 62 percent of the total construction process (Table 10), all performed by the generalized conscripts mobilized through one of the nonreciprocal labor systems outlined in the previous chapter.

My assessment of masons as laborers is that they too were part of the generalized corps of workers. Manufacturing masonry blocks is a very simple task requiring very few skills that again are highly repetitive. Eaton (1991), pointing to the distribution and morphological identification of construction tools, suggests that all households had access to fundamental construction tools, perhaps an indication that masons were commoners and generalized laborers. Similarly, Lewenstein (1987:194) describes a relative homogeneity in the spatial distribution of tool types, including those used in construction, at the Late Preclassic site of Cerros, Belize. Certainly stoneworking was conducted on the household level for basic house construction. In a sense, commoners did "prepare" cobbles for basic structures, used both for the platform retaining wall and often as a basal foundation to the superstructural wattle and daub walls. These same commoners worked on incrementally larger structures—improved structures—as part of their redistributive labor obligation to the elite within their broader social corporate unit as well as to the state. Certainly masonry skills learned during participation in lower-level construction projects were maintained through these increasing levels of labor recruitment. Finally, there is neither ideological attachment to masonry blocks nor any known rituals per se associated with masonry that would have heightened their symbolic value.

This assessment perhaps runs counter to that suggested by Becker (1973); I say "perhaps" since it may actually conform to Becker's assessment of the place of masons. Becker compares the artifact assemblage from Structure 1 in Group 4G at Tikal, a rather elaborate structure (comparable perhaps to Structure 9N-83 at Copan), with that from Structure 4 in Group 4H. Based on "twice as many" limestone smoothing tools associated with the former structure, he concludes that Structure 1 represented a "residence and probably the workshop of a family of masons or stucco workers" (ibid.:402). I am equivocal in my assessment of this conclusion since plaster manufacturers (stucco workers) likely *did* represent a household-based, specialized activity at Copan, as is discussed below. However, Becker's assessment of masons as specialists is questionable since (1) no context for the artifacts is provided, (2) no analysis beyond the morphological identification of these tools is provided, (3) absolute numbers of tools are not given, and (4) the presence of construction tools in and of itself is not a sufficient index of specialized production—certainly someone did masonry work and used an appropriate tool. The question is that of connecting artifacts to an institutional framework, and until more data are presented that clearly implicate masons as specialists, I will cluster those workers with other generalized laborers—

talented individuals nonrandomly and perhaps more frequently drawn from commoner or perhaps lower-ranking lineage administrator households. The mean percentage of time and effort expended on masonry, including procurement, transport, and manufacture, was 73 percent of the total construction process.

I would similarly include as generalized laborers many if not all of the actual builders of the improved structure—those erecting the walls and constructing the roofs. The mean percentage of time and effort in those activities was 3 percent of the total. Additional activities, such as the weaving of matted doorways, although not quantified in this study, are also considered as work performed by talented but generalized laborers.

Therefore, in my analysis, a full 87 percent of the total construction effort (derived from Table 10 and Appendix A) was expended by generalized laborers in the construction of masonry structures. These tasks account for all of the time expended in the construction process except that expended in the manufacture of plaster and sculpture. This figure of 87 percent represents the percentage of time expended by generalized labor and is almost identical to the percentage of generalized personnel calculated on the basis of actual people involved in construction (see below). This may seem high to some, but in fact there are analogs from societies with comparable if not greater economic complexity. Heather Swanson, for example, in her book *Medieval Artisans* (1989:82), states that "the magnificent churches, cathedrals and castles which survived from medieval England celebrate the achievements of the most notable builders of the time, but tend to obscure the fact that the vast majority of building workers were involved in very unspectacular tasks."

Specialized Labor: The Improved Form

Based on the criteria of skills, energy, and ideological value, I suggest, as others have (Adams 1970; Becker 1973; Haviland 1974), that the positions of architect and sculptor were filled by specialized individuals. These specialized positions, created by the elite to serve the elite, have been termed "elite" or "attached" specialists (Earle 1981). Currently there are no direct archaeological data that identify the position of architect; acceptance of such a specialized position is based on the skills and high value (both energetic and ideologic) of large-scale architecture. We do, however, have more data on sculptors, reflecting perhaps a similar institutional framework for the position of architect. Cohodas (1976:309), studying the sculpture of Yaxchilan from an art historic–stylistic perspective, concluded that the forty sculptures carved at that site in the period A.D. 752–770 represent "the work of a single innovative master carver of the Bird Jaguar period in Yaxchilan." Based on this stylistic analysis, and coupled with the ethnographic and historic data, which consistently speak of a royal or master architect in early state systems, I conclude that there existed at Copan and other large Maya polities a royal sculptor and royal architect.

In addition, it is possible that at least the larger lineage units also supported their own sculptor. Haviland (1974) presents data which, though admittedly tentative, may indicate the presence of a lineage-based sculptor. His data, from Structure 4F-3, a large residence in a courtyard outside the Main Center of Tikal, include chipped stone tools appropriate for sculpturing, a higher percentage of some lithic tools than in other middens, a higher percentage of hammerstones, fragments of carvings, and a miniature replica of a stela. Collectively these data suggest that sculpturing activities took place in this courtyard, performed by the occupant of this structure. It is possible then that, in addition to a royal sculptor, there existed lower-ranking sculptors supported by each lineage. From this it can be inferred that the structure of royal specialists was perhaps paralleled on a smaller scale by each lineage. This hypothesis could be tested at sites such as Copan—for example, a comparative artistic analysis of the sculptured façades of elite residences may distinguish the specific style(s) and thus number of attached sculptors.

I would further suggest that some bureaucratic overseer—perhaps the equivalent of an accountant—was also involved as a specialist in the construction of improved masonry structures. I include this position since documents from powerful states such as pharaonic Egypt (Bierbrier 1982:32) stress the importance of record-keeping scribes in corvée labor systems. The analysis of energy in buildings reveals that several forms of redistributive labor systems—including the corvée—existed during the Classic period. As mentioned, these systems are generally based on rotating obligatory participation; thus, records must be kept in order to monitor and schedule participation, to coordinate and record the use of materials, and perhaps to record incidentals such as injuries. I would suggest that, certainly at the highest-ranking lineage and state levels, some bureaucrat must have performed this specialized task. I would add, however, that this specific accounting task was likely to be one of several such tasks performed by this individual.

The number of individuals filling these three specialist positions was very low. As I have suggested elsewhere (Abrams 1987), there probably existed on the state level a single royal architect and a single royal sculptor, although this number is of course conjectural. The number of royal specialists energetically required could certainly be exceeded if desired, since both the product of the specialist as well as the mere existence of the specialist reflected the prestige and wealth of the ruler. However, it is likely that the number of attached sculptors at Copan was roughly equal to the number of maximal lineages plus one additional royal or master sculptor.

The energetic data, in concert with excavated features at Copan, suggest further that plasterers represented a fourth position of specialized producers associated with improved masonry structures.

In the test-pitting of the Copan pocket, a small mound (Site 70-30) was sampled (Freter 1988). Presumed initially to be a small housemound, it was revealed by excavation to be the outer earthen wall of a small kiln. Based on a 20 percent exposure, it was determined that the walls were constructed of burnt clay and formed a rounded, in-curving feature unlike any residence. The interior contents included large chunks of charred limestone, carbon, and ash; in concert with the absence of sherds within the feature and very few sherds outside the feature, it was functionally identified as a limestone calcining kiln used in the manufacture of plaster for construction.

Plaster production required several well-defined procedures. First limestone and wood had to be procured from the upland zones and transported to the kiln. The wood and then the limestone had to be correctly placed within the kiln such that burning of the wood would successfully reduce, or calcine, the limestone, which, upon absorbing oxygen, became quicklime. The addition of water produced slaked lime, and the final step involved adding an aggregate to the slaked lime to prevent extensive shrinkage. The aggregate used at Copan has been identified as tuff, with the ratio of tuff to limestone ranging between 1:1 and 1:4 (Hyman 1970). Tannic acid, perhaps extracted from the bark of various trees, was another additive to prevent extensive shrinking.

Plaster must have been manufactured immediately prior to and during the actual building process, and thus the plaster producers must have worked on a seasonal basis. The considerable technical skills required in plaster manufacture, in concert with the high energetic costs of plaster production, strongly suggest that construction plaster was produced by seasonal specialists.

Since the kiln described above is located about 1 km northeast of Las Sepulturas and adjoins a small Type 1 rural courtyard, it is presumed that all or some members of these commoner households were the operators of this

kiln and thus were the producers of construction plaster. Based on the energetic costs of plaster manufacture using the open-air method and the volumes
of plaster consumed by various large structures, an estimate of the number
of plaster manufacturers can be generated. If the operation of one kiln required essentially the entire dry season and produced roughly 10 m^3 of plaster, then Structure 10L-22, which utilized about 80 m^3 of plaster, required
the simultaneous operation of eight kilns. Structure 9N-82C, which utilized
about 40 m^3 of plaster, then required plaster from four kilns. If each kiln was
operated by the household heads within a small rural courtyard, then perhaps
four people per kiln were involved; thus thirty-two people produced the
plaster for Structure 10L-22. Similarly, sixteen people would have been involved in the actual production of plaster for Structure 9N-82C. However,
these figures may be inflated since the greater efficiency of an enclosed kiln
relative to open-air production would have lowered the number of operators.

It is possible that the ruling elite controlled some kilns for their own purposes, or perhaps demanded this material from various lineages as part of
their obligations to the state. These plaster manufacturers did produce for
the elite, but unlike the royal or attached specialist positions of architect and
sculptor, this particular position did not convey a distinctly high status.
These producers were likely subsumed within the ranks of the commoners.
Nadel (1942), in his description of specialists within the Nupe state of West
Africa, indicated that the status of attached specialists varied as a function of
the perceived ideological and material value of the product. Perhaps it could
be inferred that plaster, albeit a very important material component in architecture, had no great symbolic value for the Maya. The socioeconomic position of plaster producers is very similar to that established at Copan for
obsidian workers and possibly woodworkers (Mallory 1984), groundstone
producers (Spink 1983), utilitarian ceramic manufacturers (Freter 1991), and
chert tool producers (Valdez and Potter 1991). All are rather peripheral spatially and quite "common" socioeconomically; as argued below, these specialists represent a rather distinct sphere of production and exchange within
the broader Late Classic economy.

A final specialist position associated with elite architecture was that of
painter. Both the interior and exterior of many masonry structures were
coated with paint, and colors bore ideological significance for the Maya
(Schele 1985), as they do for most if not all societies. The manufacture of
pigments, regardless of color, was a relatively straightforward process requiring modest skills (ibid.:33). Certainly less economically complex societies have been able to produce pigments. Nonetheless, I assume that the base

for Maya paints was plaster or lime-based whitewash to which these pigments were added, and plaster was produced by seasonal specialists. In addition, colors had very high symbolic value. As a consequence, I suggest that some specialists, perhaps overlapping with plasterers, were responsible for the manufacture and application of paints.

One category of specialized laborers that some may feel has been neglected is that of the foreman or on-site overseer of the actual construction of masonry structures, which required greater skills. The architect personally supervised and inspected the work in progress, bearing ultimate responsibility for the project's success. In addition, there were likely lower-level supervisory positions. However, these positions were probably filled by generalized laborers who simply possessed greater knowledge and skills than others and who had higher social status (but not power) within the commoner segment of society. I have been explicit in stating that not all generalized laborers were equally skilled in construction and that generalized laborers, conscripted within some form of a redistributive labor system, were recruited from commoner households in a nonrandom manner based on social corporate affiliation, past participation, and likely a range of particularistic and historic circumstances. These points logically imply that household or courtyard heads who possessed greater skills and respect would de facto assume greater responsibilities in terms of leadership and orchestration of the work of kin. These same individuals working together in construction similarly worked together in agricultural tasks and other familial affairs. Again, if decisions were made based on their comparative efficiencies, the position of construction supervisor would simply have been created within the pre-existing structure of social relations.

Collectively, several specialist positions can be inferred primarily from the assessment of skill, energetics, and ideological value of the range of tasks in construction. As an exercise, the number of generalized and specialized personnel can be generated from the energetic data. Taking Structure 10L-22 as an example, I calculate that 263 generalized laborers were involved in construction, assuming a sixty-day work period per task, which translates into about one hundred days per project (assuming linearity of tasks; derived from Appendix A with all fractions rounded up). It was suggested earlier that about 32 laborers were involved in plaster production for Structure 10L-22. If one master sculptor assisted by nine apprentices and one master architect and accountant were involved, then approximately 45 specialized laborers participated in this construction project. In total, 308 laborers participated, 15 percent of whom would be categorized as specialized personnel. This same set of calculations was conducted for several large masonry structures, and similar ratios were produced. Structure 9N-82C, for example, would have required a total of 129 laborers, 19 (or 15 percent) of whom would have been specialists. As with Structure 10L-22, the majority of these specialists were involved in plaster production, which represented a mean of 13 percent of the total cost of improved construction. If future research confirms that this figure is inflated (being based on open-air production rather than kilns), the percentage of generalized personnel would increase to well above 90 percent of the total work force.

A final consideration of elite or attached specialists involves a discussion of the system of training of some of these specialists. All specialists were not alike, and there were subdivisions within each category. Here I will consider the system of training as it affected attached specialists comparable to the position of architect and sculptor. Based on what might be considered an ethnological analog, I consider the training of these specialists within a system of apprenticeships. This system is generally designed to educate a small number of individuals to perform special economic tasks. It is distinct from household education or mass education in that only some individuals within society receive such experiential training and that the training often involves the transmission of "secret" knowledge from a master to an apprentice. Furthermore, training involves not just the learning of technical skills, but also codes of conduct in both the economic and social domains (Coy 1989). The sculptural analysis at Yaxchilan pointed to the conclusion that "at some Maya sites, it appears that sculptors may have been aided by apprentices in the carving of glyphs and less significant detail" (Cohodas 1976:312). Presumably lineage sculptors, lower in rank than the royal sculptor, trained fewer apprentices (if any); these apprentices perhaps achieved a status that was above that of the commoner but still low within the ranks of the lineage or secondary elite. It is not known from which ranks apprentices were drawn. Based on sculpture fragments spanning many chronological stages of construction history of Structure 4F-3, Haviland (1974:496) suggests that such positions were hereditary. If so, then apprentices were presumably drawn from equivalent ranks of the elite, perhaps a component of the endogamous structure of the Maya elite.

The Scale of Economic Specialization

One of the direct conclusions concerning economic specialization, *specific to construction personnel,* was that a relatively modest degree of specialization was necessary for the construction of very elaborate and costly architecture. Very few individuals actually filled specialized positions, with the vast majority of construction personnel being represented by generalized conscripts. Although analyses based on lithic goods and commodities designed to reconstruct the scale of economic complexity correctly stress the organizational variability among Maya polities (Shafer and Hester 1986), there is likely no such comparable degree of variability in the scale of construction positions. This suggestion of limited variability among Maya sites is based essentially on the nature of the product—the house. Whether basic or improved, the demand for this domestic product is limited and directly related to the number of household units at any site. In addition, it is a product which, relative to other goods, involved high energy expenditure, thus requiring collective social behaviors for its creation. Finally, architecture is not a commodity, or a product created explicitly for exchange, and thus no sites could produce houses for export as they could for smaller and less costly goods (here I am discounting intergenerational exchange, or inheritance). These factors collectively tend to minimize the intersite variability in the organization and scale of specialization concerning construction personnel.

Notwithstanding, some degree of variability existed among Maya centers. In fact, the logical underpinning of the analysis of labor systems and specialization is that the scale of organizational complexity correlates with the overall scale of social power. Thus at Tikal, where a relatively expansive sociopolitical hierarchy was established (for example, with greater numbers of lineage administrative levels), a greater number of lineage sculptors and other associated personnel would have existed. In addition, site-specific environmental settings would have affected to some degree the scale of specialization. The production of lime-plaster, for example, exhibited considerable variability in terms of production technology and raw-material access, and thus the scale and structure of these construction personnel would have varied.

Ultimately, the low level of specialization regarding construction personnel correlates with the demands of the product and the demand sector consuming the product of these specialists (Abrams 1987:494–495). In terms of demand, houses and other architecture were relatively high-cost, low-consumption products. In terms of the demand sector, all of the actual construction specialist positions were created explicitly for the production of improved residential structures or large-scale civic architecture, and thus may be considered specialists attached to or retained by the elite (whether state or lineage). Although these factors converge to produce four or five specialist positions, few people actually filled each of these positions; thus the number of positions and the number of people filling those positions become distinct and important analytic units of comparison. Hypothetically, the earliest stages of economic specialization should be characterized by (1) the expansion in the number of specialists producing for the elite (i.e., retainers) relative to those producing for society at large and (2) a relatively low number of specialists filling each retained position. This analysis then supports the conclusion of other researchers (e.g., Aldenderfer, Kimball, and Sievert 1989; Hendon 1991) that a rather preliminary stage of economic specialization may have characterized the broader economy of the Classic Maya.

The Structure of Economic Specialization

It is inevitable that research assessing scale will demonstrate variability among goods produced within the Classic Maya economy. I am in fact very cautious about projecting the *scale* of economic specialization for architecture to other goods and do so, first, to present the empirical data and conclusions concerning that one specific good and, second, to offer a comparative springboard for similar analyses of different goods. Only after a large number of such analyses are conducted will the complexities of production fully emerge. I am less hesitant, however, to project the *organizational structure* as reconstructed for construction to other products within the Maya economy. Following the analogous (if not homologous) principles of the evolution of cultural systems based on comparative efficiencies, we should be able to propose some systemic organization of production and distribution of goods and services that similarly subsumed both architecture and some other goods within Maya society. The analysis of architecture yields two general organizational structures: (1) a reciprocal system of labor exchange among households conducted within the Domestic Mode of Production and (2) a redistributive system, with varying forms and degrees of balance, integrating the commoner household level with more hierarchic administrative levels. Within the reciprocal system, a relatively symmetric exchange of labor and skills involved socioeconomic equals in a rather broad spatial network; this system was effectively responsible for the production of the vast majority of houses built by the Classic Copan Maya. The production system operated as it does in relatively egalitarian societies described in the anthropological literature. Despite the fact that skills varied, this horizontal structure of production did not require economic specialists (or very few contracted specialists), but rather generalists of considerable knowledge and practical skills. The redistributive system, which connected commoners to several administrative levels of the lineage and state, was responsible for producing elite artifacts in the form of masonry structures for consumption by the elite. Although specialist positions were created, very few individuals were actually involved in this more vertical structure of production, given the rates of production and consumption of those goods and the characteristics of the elite as a demand sector.

Collectively, this determination of various specific loci of production and exchange, representing systems of instituted economic behaviors, best conforms to the model of "multiple spheres of exchange" within economic anthropology (Bohanan 1959). According to this model, various socioeconomic units are responsible for producing specific types and numbers of goods and services, with the exchange of these commodities orchestrated through very specific and restrictive channels. In addition, distinct social and ideological traditions and perceptions are associated with each specific sphere of exchange. The production and distribution of goods would be structured as follows: some utilitarian artifacts would be produced by households and exchanged within a reciprocal system; others would be produced by lineage specialists, distributed only to lineage members. Elite goods would be produced by attached lineage specialists for consumption by maximal lineage heads or circulated from the maximal lineage heads to the king within a specific sphere of exchange among the more powerful elite. Intersite exchange among elites would represent a spatial extension of the elite exchange sphere. The main point here is that this economic model is supported by the architectural energetic data, suggesting that this model may be valuable in examining the production and distribution of other goods and services within the Classic Maya economy as well as other archaeological economies (e.g., Hirth 1984).

Furthermore, this basic model of multiple and distinct social centers of production and spheres of exchange can be subsumed within a more powerful and overarching model. Karl Polanyi (1957) offered the concept of "social embeddedness" as characterizing the economy of all early states. Polanyi's model of the early state economy was one that emphasized reciprocal and redistributive organizational structures as the primary if not exclusive means for the material provisioning of society. These economic structures were created within the context of preexisting *social* structures, such as households, lineages, and other social corporate units. The entire economic analysis of architectural construction leads me to conclude that the orchestration of personnel, the exchanges of labor, the creation of specialists, and the differential access to labor were all established within and guided by the structure of the sociopolitical hierarchy of power.

This is not an argument that "social institutions" cause "economic institutions," or some similar unilineal, monocausal explanation. Rather, the existence and influence of multiple complex cultural interactions leading to new or modified institutions is fully recognized. Relatively early in Maya prehistory, there were very solid infrastructural variables such as population increase, a sedentary economic base, and diminishing resources through time, which led to the establishment and selection of social corporate units such as lineages. Once established, however, these institutions exerted profound influence on the continuing cultural selection process. Until these institutions become ineffective as mechanisms for the provisioning of society, they will probabilistically endure. All of the architectural data and evolutionary models strongly converge on the conclusion that economic activities were principally embedded within the sociopolitical structure.

I emphasize the importance of this model for several reasons. First, it appears to conform best to the hierarchic structure of the energetic data. Second, this model of social relations of production, with emphasis on the lack of separation between social and economic behaviors, is theoretically and ethnologically supported (cf. Sahlins 1972). Third, it clearly deemphasizes the role of market systems operating according to the market principle as the primary institution of economic exchange. Finally, the relative amounts of energy exchanged through each distinct sphere may serve as a measure of economic complexity and a springboard for future comparative analyses.

A final point in the discussion of economics and architecture concerns this question of the relative amounts of energy, goods, or services flowing through distinct spheres or channels of exchange. Specifically, there has been considerable debate centered on the amount of labor provided by the commoners to the elite for construction purposes. The structure of this exchange, expressed in the form of various redistributive systems, including the corvée system, has been established and discussed in Chapter 7. However, the *amount* of labor moving through this commoner-elite sphere of exchange has long been assumed to be very high during the Late Classic period, and this presumed overtaxation of construction labor has then been causally linked with the Classic Maya collapse. J. Eric Thompson, the originator of this argument, stated, "It is not illogical to suppose that there was a series of peasant revolts against the theocratic minority of priests . . . and nobles. This may have been caused by the ever growing demands for service in construction work and in the production of food for an increasing number of nonproducers" (1954:105). In a more recent study, Hosler, Sabloff, and Runge

(1977) have simulated the political collapse of Maya polities, concluding that political competition for construction labor led to overtaxation, triggering systemic failure (but cf. Watson, LeBlanc, and Redman 1984:96 for a critique of this simulation).

Based on the assumption that the number of laborers conscripted in the construction of Structure 10L-22—perhaps a maximum of 300—represents a typical annual amount of drafted commoner laborers, the present analysis has demonstrated that the labor contribution or tax to the ruling elite, *on an annual household basis,* was not high in absolute and relative terms. Collectively, each household head may have contributed service to all levels of the elite once every few years, and, of course, certain benefits or resources moved down from the elite as part of this exchange equation (Webster 1985). Again, the conspicuous nature of architecture in the archaeological record, reflecting but one component of exchange, tends to obfuscate the more complex and dynamic exchange systems that existed between commoners and elites.

This conclusion may undergo revision; when more structures are quantified, particularly in the urban centers, researchers may estimate an annual investment of labor far beyond that which I have generated from my sample. However, until that time, the best approximation of labor taxation for construction is that presented here, and it is incumbent upon archaeologists to apply architectural energetics if they are to substantively revise this conclusion.

9

Conclusions

The present research has applied the methodological and analytical potential of architectural energetics to buildings constructed by the ancient Copan Maya. This research is part of a growing body of literature addressing the means through which archaeologists define architectural scale. This is done in three basic ways: (1) subjective assessment, (2) comparative metric and volumetric measurements, and (3) energetic quantification.

The first involves classification based on impressions of observed size, yielding descriptions such as "huge," "massive," and "monumental." A central goal of the present work has been to encourage archaeologists to transcend this highly subjective and analytically empty descriptive approach. The second approach involves the estimation of various metric, areal, or volumetric dimensions of buildings, such as height of the substructure, basal platform area, or volume of fill. In its varied forms, this approach is an extremely valuable step beyond the subjective, as demonstrated by various analyses.

The third approach is termed architectural energetics and involves the translation of architecture into an energy equivalence, expressed here in a standard currency of labor-time. The methodology and application was presented for the Maya site of Copan, Honduras. A representative sample of fully excavated structures from this site was quantified in terms of construction cost, with these comparative costs serving as the basis for various analyses of Classic Maya institutions. The quantification translated architecture into volumes of materials and then translated these volumes into energy costs, expressed in person-days. A set of replicative experiments, most of which were specific to Copan, served as the basis for determining labor costs for each task in the construction process.

It was argued that this approach has the potential to provide a more powerful quantified analytic measure of any structure or building episode than can any of the specific volumetric measurements. This statement is not without its qualifications. The ability to apply architectural energetics is dependent upon the quality of architectural data, and thus each researcher must evaluate which method of quantification is appropriate for the architecture being studied. Furthermore, given specific research questions, an energetic quantification may not provide greater insights than those from a simpler volumetric quantification. No method of quantification is better in the absolute. Nonetheless, architectural energetics represents a stage in the continuum of specificity in quantification, and the present application of architectural energetics has, I hope, demonstrated its far-reaching potential for more detailed analyses of past societies.

The present energetic study quantified a wide range of structures from Copan that had been thoroughly excavated, principally through the efforts of the PAC II project. Given the scale of that project, the body of data concerning buildings was enviable, making possible not only volumetric evaluations but also the energetic estimates, coupling the volumes with costs per task derived primarily from replicative studies. In many ways, the quality of architectural data from an archaeological site could be evaluated in terms of its energetic quantifiability.

Although the method of quantification could be applied to any type of structure, the present study focused on housing as a unit of architectural analysis rather than the broader set of structures subsumed within architecture. This decision was made simply on the basis of the analytic questions in mind, which ultimately were conceived to serve as an illustration and justification of the method. It was felt that measurements of relative social power, labor systems, and economic specialization were best reflected in the differential energy expended in a range of houses (some of which are in fact "monumental") rather than other or more inclusive categories of architecture. This subjective analytic decision is in no way meant to minimize or contradict analyses that use alternative architectural samples or, as stated above, alternative quantitative approaches. Furthermore, this energetic analysis of housing is seen as complementary to nonenergetic analyses of architecture. There is absolutely no reason why architectural studies of, say, geomancy should be considered antithetical to this study.

In presenting the methodology of architectural energetics, I have tried to be as explicit as possible since such clarity is an essential characteristic of energetic studies. This means, of course, that both the strengths and short-comings of the data must be presented with equal clarity if they are to serve as the foundation for future refinements. The present study recognizes that "true" costs will never be known, a consequence of studying the unobserv-able past. In that sense, any specific numbers in this study are secondary to the goal of making architecture as quantified as possible as part of our com-plete analytic exploitation of the archaeological record.

Several substantive conclusions were reached based on the energetic quan-tification of residential architecture at Copan. For heuristic purposes, two categories of housing—the basic and the improved forms—were presented. Although there is an empirical continuum between these forms, the former was defined as perishable structures on relatively low substructural plat-forms, and the latter was defined as houses bearing masonry superstructural walls. After discussing these two forms of housing, it was suggested that, in addition to their greater symbolic value, improved residential structures pro-vided their occupants with an enhanced biopsychological quality of life, par-ticularly in terms of health and comfort. Commoners viewing these elite structures saw more than symbols of power; they saw better housing and better living conditions, and it was suggested that these latter realities con-firmed and reified, if not generated, those more symbolic perceptions.

A general, macro-societal model of the segmentary state, expressed more specifically as the lineage model, was supported by the energetic data. This model is characterized by a stratified elite representing the power of the state and of various maximal lineage units. This stratified elite occupied about 5 percent of the houses at Late Classic Copan. A ranked secondary elite, comprised of the households of lineage administrators and their attached spe-cialists, represented three subordinate tiers in terms of social power and oc-cupied about 10 percent of the houses. Collectively, then, 15 percent of all houses were associated in some manner with the elite segment of Late Classic Copan society. The largest segment of society consisted of commoners, con-stituting approximately 85 percent of all households. Based on the con-tinuum of costs, it was argued that the rural and urban commoners were all structured within lineages of varying power and rank.

This hierarchy of social power and energy served as the basis for testing ethnographic models of labor organization for house construction. It was concluded that various reciprocal and redistributive labor systems existed at Classic Copan, increasing in overall complexity and energy upward through the social hierarchy. Although a corvée system of labor recruitment was suggested for royal structures, it was argued that the scale of labor taxation for construction by the state was relatively modest and clearly distinct from oppressive conscriptive systems within many historic empires.

Finally, it was concluded that several specialist positions were required for the construction of large-scale architecture, including the positions of architect, sculptor, accountant, plasterer, and painter. It was argued that these positions were "attached specialists," supported on the basis of power within the sociopolitical hierarchy. Thus, the state supported more of these positions than a single lineage of modest social ranking. It was further suggested that these positions were not all of equal social status and that, except for plasterers, relatively few individuals filled these positions. It is difficult to offer a simple categorization of the Classic Maya economy since economic complexity is a continuum measured by several factors, and this analysis is restricted to inferences based on architecture. Nonetheless, all of the reconstructions generated in this study conclude that many if not all of the economic activities conducted by the Classic Maya were organized, structured, and "embedded" within the hierarchic matrix of statuses of the lineage model. This suggests that the bulk of productive activities was orchestrated on the household and lineage level and that various forms of reciprocity and redistribution served as the primary mechanisms of provisioning society with those goods and services.

These analyses have been guided by the theoretical principles within the paradigm of cultural materialism and cultural selection, which I effectively collapse into one category. I need not review here those central principles (discussed in Chapter 3), which contemporary theoretical architects such as Marvin Harris (1979) have already outlined with great clarity and force. I will simply note that these theories are viewed as inclusive rather than exclusive frameworks for understanding the past, their theoretical power reflected in their ability to prioritize factors that influence a wide range of human behaviors and thoughts and to guide research, exemplified by the present study.

One aspect of archaeological reconstruction that I have stressed in this study is the heavy use of ethnographic analogs in their role as models against which empirical data must be presented. The use of ethnographic models was an essential component in the process of reconstruction. All of the models in this study are testable, although not all were tested here. For example, the capturing of water from roofs, discussed in Chapter 5, was suggested based on analogy but was not tested. Detailed ceramic analysis, however, could potentially serve as a test of that analog. I accentuate the use of analogs since archaeology becomes a rather shallow endeavor when isolated from ethnography.

Comparative Studies of Architectural Energetics

The application of architectural energetics here has been site-specific since the method of quantification demands such specificity. However, as was stated in Chapter 1, architectural energetics can be applied on a pansocietal basis. In this concluding section, I will offer a comparison of various representative applications, which will, I hope, make clearer the development of architectural energetics and offer guidelines for future research.

A large proportion of the research directed at quantifying architecture in an archaeological context has focused on large public structures in both state and prestate systems. Examples of such research in prestate systems include the quantification of borrows, mounds, and henges in England (Renfrew 1973, 1983; Startin 1982; Earle 1991), various mounds in the midwestern United States (Aaberg and Bonsignore 1975; Reed, Bennett, and Porter 1968), kivas in the southwestern United States (Lekson 1984), and *heiau* in Hawaii (Kolb 1991). Principally these studies have yielded important substantive conclusions concerning territoriality, group interaction and cooperative exchange, and the comparative power of the emergent elite. Certainly more such studies are needed with these same research questions in mind.

One very intriguing aspect of the quantification of public structures in prestate systems is the demonstrated high levels of energy expended by these "low-energy" societies. The cost of building the Poverty Point complex, a set of Archaic earthworks located in northeastern Louisiana, is estimated to be approximately 1.4 million p-d (Aaberg and Bonsignore 1975:60). According to Startin (1982:155), the cost of constructing the late Neolithic Silbury Hill is estimated at 500,000 p-d. One of the better-controlled architectural energetic studies quantified the construction of Hawaiian *heiau*, or shrines, within a range of chiefdoms (Kolb 1991). Although most construction events cost less than a few thousand person-days, some ranged beyond 10,000 p-d, the highest costing 55,469 p-d (ibid.:162). These and other analyses (e.g., Kaplan 1963; Erasmus 1965; Pozorski 1980) not only demonstrate the high levels of cumulative energy expended by prestate societies, but also have the following implications in the application of architectural energetics: (1) large public structures are more likely to be constructed over longer periods of time than are residential structures and (2) the estimate of energy expended in public structures will have limited (but some) analytic value if viewed in a noncomparative manner—that is, in isolation from other similarly quantified structures.

Residential architecture has rarely been quantified in an egalitarian context (Callahan 1981). In my opinion, energetics will have the greatest anthropological import when applied to ranked or stratified systems (Peebles and Kus 1977), exemplified by the energetic quantification of pueblos in Chaco Canyon (Lekson 1984).

Similarly, relatively few architectural energetic studies have been applied to public architecture in state systems, with research in the Maya region being the notable exception. However, those public structures that have been quantified reveal the extremely high amounts of energy capable of being expended. For example, the Pyramid of the Sun in Teotihuacan, Mexico, has been estimated to have required 10,000,000 p-d (Aaberg and Bonsignore 1975). The numerous pyramids built between ca. 2700 B.C. and 2400 B.C. in Egypt required a constant seasonal (three months) labor input of 70,000 men (Mendelssohn 1974:143). Storey (1992:461) has quantified several large public works from state systems, the most costly being the Great Wall of China, estimated to have required 328,383 person-years.

In the present study, Structure 10L-22 was taken to represent the upper end in annual expenditure in residential structures. Its estimated cost of about 25,000 p-d may represent, by order of magnitude, the upper end of labor taxation in construction on an annual basis. However, even if other structures, once quantified, are shown to be somewhat greater in cost (which in fact I expect), by comparison with other state systems, the Classic Maya structures will still remain intermediate in cost and annual labor input between egalitarian societies and the immensely powerful civilizations of the past.

Research concerning residential structures in state systems has by and large been restricted to Mayan studies, applied at Uxmal (Erasmus 1965), Tikal (Arnold and Ford 1980), Copan (Abrams 1984a, 1987; Gonlin 1985, 1993), Coba (Folan et al. 1982), the Belize River Valley (Ford 1991), and Sayil (Carmean 1991). These studies not only demonstrate the value of architectural energetics on a site-specific level, but also suggest its potential for intrasite analyses, especially in terms of measuring social power. Interestingly, despite the fact that site-specific costs are used and methods of quantification vary, there is a clear comparability among costs. For example, Structure 9N-82-C at Copan was estimated to have cost approximately 10,000 p-d (discounting reuse). Platform 87 at Sayil, which included the residence of a high-status household, has been estimated to have cost 7,136 p-d (Carmean 1991:159), a quite comparable figure. Similarly, Arnold and Ford (1980:724) suggest that the structures representing the subroyal elite at Tikal range from 109 p-d to 19,000 p-d. The convergence of these figures is strongly suggestive of the analytic potential of architectural energetics.

Future Research

A central goal of this work has been to encourage other researchers to include the energetic quantification of architecture in their inventory of standard descriptions of the archaeological material culture. If this approach is pursued, there are two primary areas for future development and research: (1) the expansion and improvement of energetic costs and (2) the more complete exploration of analytic applications both within and among sites.

The first area for future research requires that archaeologists be willing to conduct a battery of replicative experiments to generate or augment energetic costs from a particular site or region. As we know, costs per task will vary among sites, and thus many more estimates are required. In addition to replicative experiments, more ethnoarchaeological studies of contemporary house construction and associated household data are needed. The ethnographic data should include all aspects of house construction—such as labor organization and seasonality of construction—as well as data concerning household size, household structure, and food production activities (cf. Wilk 1991). I cannot overemphasize the need to study contemporary housing from the perspective of family health quality. The replicative experiments and the ethnographic studies are neither particularly costly nor time-consuming; if they are not designed as a specific project, perhaps they can be conducted to some degree as adjuncts to larger archaeological projects.

The expansion and improvement of the quality of architectural energetic data should then be compiled for easy reference so that researchers can access such data quickly. Perhaps a compendium of energetic data embracing a wider range of activities, such as agricultural, manufacturing, and transportation costs, is required for a more effective and complete application of energetics in Maya archaeology.

Researchers should bear in mind that energetic costs need not be site-specific, in the strict sense that costs be derived from that particular site. The data needed to translate architecture into energy, however, must be site-appropriate. Thus, costs estimated from other areas but with comparable technoenvironmental conditions should be applicable. Nonetheless, I would still stress the need of generating cost data in the field when possible.

The present application, in concert with other energetic studies, has focused on issues of social power relations, the organization of labor, and varied economic components related to construction. In my opinion, the issue of reconstructing social power relations, especially in ranked and stratified societies, will likely represent the dominant analytic focus of architectural energetics and should be pursued as completely as possible at all archaeological sites. Once accomplished, the comparative structure of social power on a regional and interregional basis becomes possible. Further analyses beyond those of social power should be explored in the future. Settlement patterns, for example, could be described in terms of the distribution of energy (and concomitant power) rather than in numbers and densities of structures. When costs are determined for similar tasks in different regions, aspects of economic organization may become clearer. In addition, measuring the evolution of expenditure in public and private architecture still remains one of the most valuable empirical measures of social complexity available to archaeologists.

As more archaeologists consider the use of architectural energetics, regardless of where they are working, the value of this approach will become more apparent. I hope the present study, in both method and results, contributes in some way toward that end, ultimately helping archaeologists generate a better understanding of ancient societies.

Appendix A.
Costs per Task
per Structure

Costs (expressed in p-d) are cumulative costs per structure minus any savings through reuse. Cumulative costs are the sum of Appendices A and B (see Table 7).

Structure 10L-22 = 24,705

Procurement		Transport		Manufacture		Construction	
earth	490	earth	673	masonry	3,411	walls	556
cobbles	263	cobbles	4,075	plaster	5,156	fill	35
tuff	1,978	tuff	4,041	sculpture	2,404	cobbled surface	45
		plaster	1,554			plaster surface	24
	2,731		10,343		10,971		660

Structure 9N-82-C = 8,567

Procurement		Transport		Manufacture		Construction	
earth	38	earth	103	masonry	1,882	walls	218
cobbles	24	cobbles	145	plaster	1,699	fill	47
tuff	562	tuff	2,868	sculpture	95	cobbled surface	17
		plaster	774			plaster surface	95
	624		3,890		3,676		377

Structure 9N-82-E = 7,491

Procurement		Transport		Manufacture		Construction	
earth	27	earth	91	masonry	1,407	walls	152
cobbles	24	cobbles	152	plaster	1,670	fill	30
tuff	540	tuff	2,756			cobbled surface	9
		plaster	572			plaster surface	61
	591		3,571		3,077		252

Structure 9N-82-W = 2,361 (superstructure only)

Procurement		Transport		Manufacture		Construction	
earth	13	earth	18	masonry	590	walls	64
tuff	227	tuff	1,156	plaster	180	fill	11
		plaster	82			plaster surface	20
	240		1,256		770		95

Structure 9N-83 = 5,893

Procurement		Transport		Manufacture		Construction	
earth	94	earth	129	masonry	1,062	walls	114
cobbles	43	cobbles	267	plaster	1,084	fill	36
tuff	407	tuff	2,080	sculpture	2	cobbled surface	15
		plaster	494			plaster surface	66
	544		2,970		2,148		231

Structure 9N-81 = 1,007 (original structure)

Procurement		Transport		Manufacture		Construction	
earth	51	earth	71	masonry	165	walls	18
cobbles	18	cobbles	113	plaster	81	fill	4
tuff	63	tuff	324			cobbled surface	11
		plaster	37			plaster surface	2
						superstructure	47
	132		545		246		84

Structure 9N-81-terrace = 1,536

Procurement		Transport		Manufacture		Construction	
earth	74	earth	102	masonry	288	walls	31
cobbles	26	cobbles	164	plaster	105	fill	6
tuff	110	tuff	564			cobbled surface	14
		plaster	48			plaster surface	3
	210		878		393		54

Structure 9N-81-sub-1 = 769 (first L-shaped substructure)

Procurement		Transport		Manufacture		Construction	
earth	23	earth	31	masonry	154	walls	17
cobbles	9	cobbles	58	plaster	69	fill	6
tuff	51	tuff	303			cobbled surface	15
		plaster	32			plaster surface	2
	83		424		223		40

Structure 9N–81–sub–2 = 1,052 (second L-shaped substructure)

Procurement		Transport		Manufacture		Construction	
earth	63	earth	87	masonry	165	walls	18
cobbles	23	cobbles	144	plaster	96	fill	3
tuff	63	tuff	323			cobbled surface	20
		plaster	44			plaster surface	3
	149		598		261		44

Structure 9N–80 = 1,903

Procurement		Transport		Manufacture		Construction	
earth	55	earth	76	masonry	444	walls	37
cobbles	14	cobbles	87	plaster	491	cobbled surface	7
tuff	93	tuff	479			plaster surface	1
		plaster	21			superstructure	96
	164		663		935		141

Structure 9M–195–B = 5,058

Procurement		Transport		Manufacture		Construction	
earth	52	earth	72	masonry	1,172	walls	126
cobbles	23	cobbles	333	plaster	616	fill	26
tuff	450	tuff	1,836	sculpture	29	cobbled surface	8
		plaster	280			plaster surface	35
	525		2,521		1,817		195

Structure 9M–195–A = 160

Procurement		Transport				Construction	
earth	30	earth	41			walls	16
cobbles	3	cobbles	47			fill	2
						cobbled surface	8
						champa	13
	33		88				39

Structure 9M–194–B = 2,761

Procurement		Transport		Manufacture		Construction	
earth	26	earth	35	masonry	592	walls	64
cobbles	9	cobbles	133	plaster	483	fill	12
tuff	227	tuff	927	sculpture	1	cobbled surface	5
		plaster	220			plaster surface	27
	262		1,315		1,076		108

Structure 9M–194–A = 39

Procurement		Transport		Manufacture		Construction	
earth	4	earth	6	cobbles	6	walls	4
cobbles	1	cobbles	14			fill	1
						cobbled surface	2
						champa	1
	5		20		6		8

Structure 9M–193–B = 676

Procurement		Transport		Manufacture		Construction	
earth	21	earth	43	masonry	62	walls	66
cobbles	22	cobbles	315	plaster	38	fill	8
		plaster	17			cobbled surface	9
						plaster surface	8
						superstructure	67
	43		375		100		158

Structure 9M–193–A = 422

Procurement		Transport		Manufacture		Construction	
earth	17	earth	23	cobbles	37	walls	40
cobbles	13	cobbles	182	plaster	37	fill	5
		plaster	17			cobbled surface	5
						plaster surface	5
						superstructure	41
	30		222		74		96

Structure 9M–199 = 2,861

Procurement		Transport		Manufacture		Construction	
earth	21	earth	29	masonry	661	walls	71
cobbles	9	cobbles	128	plaster	421	fill	11
tuff	254	tuff	1,036			cobbled surface	5
		plaster	192			plaster surface	23
	284		1,385		1,082		110

Structure 9M–197 = 1,603

Procurement		Transport		Manufacture		Construction	
earth	66	earth	91	masonry	302	walls	33
cobbles	15	cobbles	224	plaster	113	fill	10
tuff	116	tuff	473			cobbled surface	11
		plaster	56			plaster surface	28
						superstructure	65
	197		844		415		147

Structure 9M-200 = 30

Procurement		Transport		Manufacture		Construction	
earth	3	earth	4	cobbles	3	walls	3
cobbles	1	cobbles	13			cobbled surface	2
						champa	1
	4		17		3		6

Structure 9M-242 = 18

Procurement		Transport		Manufacture		Construction	
earth	1	earth	1	stones	5	walls	5
		cobbles	4			cobbled surface	1
						champa	1
	1		5		5		7

Structure 9M-244 = 20

Procurement		Transport		Manufacture		Construction	
earth	3	earth	4	cobbles	1	walls	1
cobbles	1	cobbles	7			fill	1
						cobbled surface	1
						champa	1
	4		11		1		4

Structure 9M-245-A = 11

Procurement		Transport		Manufacture		Construction	
earth	1	earth	2	cobbles	1	walls	1
		cobbles	4			cobbled surface	1
						champa	1
	1		6		1		3

Structure 9M-245-B = 158

Procurement		Transport		Manufacture		Construction	
earth	3	earth	9	cobbles	4	walls	6
cobbles	3	cobbles	43	plaster	29	fill	1
		plaster	13			cobbled surface	5
						plaster surface	1
						superstructure	41
	6		65		33		54

Structure 9M-246 = 105

Procurement		Transport		Manufacture		Construction	
earth	3	earth	4	cobbles	2	walls	3
cobbles	2	cobbles	22	plaster	18	cobbled surface	2
		plaster	8			superstructure	41
	5		34		20		46

Structure 9M-196 = 101

Procurement		Transport		Manufacture		Construction	
earth	5	earth	7	cobbles	1	walls	1
cobbles	1	cobbles	27	plaster	20	fill	1
		plaster	10			plaster surface	5
						superstructure	23
	6		44		21		30

Structure 9M-189 = 986

Procurement		Transport		Manufacture		Construction	
earth	30	earth	42	masonry	205	walls	22
cobbles	11	cobbles	154	plaster	66	fill	7
tuff	79	tuff	322			cobbled surface	6
		plaster	30			plaster surface	2
						superstructure	10
	120		548		271		47

Structure 9M-191-N = 504

Procurement		Transport		Manufacture		Construction	
earth	17	earth	23	masonry	52	walls	11
cobbles	8	cobbles	109	cobbles	5	fill	5
tuff	20	tuff	82	plaster	79	cobbled surface	7
		plaster	36			plaster surface	2
						superstructure	48
	45		250		136		73

Structure 9M-192 = 452

Procurement		Transport		Manufacture		Construction	
earth	36	earth	49	plaster	11	steps	5
cobbles	17	cobbles	251			fill	8
		plaster	5			cobbled surface	5
						plaster surface	1
						superstructure	64
	53		305		11		83

Structure 9M-191-W = 191

Procurement		Transport		Manufacture		Construction	
earth	11	earth	15	cobbles	10	walls	10
cobbles	6	cobbles	89	plaster	22	fill	3
		plaster	10			cobbled surface	4
						plaster surface	1
						superstructure	10
	17		114		32		28

Structure 9M-240 = 92

Procurement		Transport		Manufacture		Construction	
earth	8	earth	11	plaster	3	walls	5
cobbles	2	cobbles	22			cobbled surface	3
		plaster	1			plaster surface	1
						superstructure	36
	10		34		3		45

Structure 9M-241 = 98

Procurement		Transport		Manufacture		Construction	
earth	4	earth	5	cobbles	9	walls	10
cobbles	2	cobbles	34	plaster	2	plaster surface	1
		plaster	1			superstructure	30
	6		40		11		41

Structure 9M-190 = 72

Procurement		Transport		Manufacture		Construction	
earth	6	earth	8	cobbles	2	walls	2
cobbles	2	cobbles	35			cobbled surface	3
						superstructure	14
	8		43		2		19

Structure 9N-67 = 4,477

Procurement		Transport		Manufacture		Construction	
earth	19	earth	27	masonry	1,165	walls	126
cobbles	8	cobbles	46	plaster	233	fill	10
tuff	447	tuff	2,281			cobbled surface	7
		plaster	106			plaster surface	2
	474		2,460		1,398		145

Structure 9N-73 = 3,429

Procurement		Transport		Manufacture		Construction	
earth	29	earth	40	masonry	727	walls	78
cobbles	14	cobbles	84	plaster	492	fill	7
tuff	279	tuff	1,425			cobbled surface	26
		plaster	224			plaster surface	4
	322		1,773		1,219		115

Structure 9N-68 = 2,199

Procurement		Transport		Manufacture		Construction	
earth	24	earth	33	masonry	545	walls	59
cobbles	9	cobbles	54	plaster	127	fill	5
tuff	209	tuff	1,068			cobbled surface	6
		plaster	58			plaster surface	2
	242		1,213		672		72

Structure 9N-74-B = 2,101

Procurement		Transport		Manufacture		Construction	
earth	14	earth	20	masonry	537	walls	67
cobbles	6	cobbles	36	plaster	132	fill	6
tuff	206	tuff	1,052			cobbled surface	7
		plaster	17			plaster surface	1
	226		1,125		669		81

Structure 9N-74-C = 1,819

Procurement		Transport		Manufacture		Construction	
earth	12	earth	17	masonry	294	walls	48
cobbles	5	cobbles	31	plaster	448	fill	5
tuff	113	tuff	635			cobbled surface	6
		plaster	204			plaster surface	1
	130		887		742		60

Structure 9N-74-A = 1,479

Procurement		Transport		Manufacture		Construction	
earth	15	earth	20	masonry	346	walls	53
cobbles	6	cobbles	36	plaster	114	fill	5
tuff	126	tuff	697			cobbled surface	8
		plaster	52			plaster surface	1
	147		805		460		67

Structure 9N-75 = 266

Procurement		Transport		Manufacture		Construction	
earth	8	earth	11	cobbles	4	walls	8
cobbles	3	cobbles	20	masonry	37	fill	1
tuff	14	tuff	73	plaster	35	cobbled surface	5
		plaster	16			plaster surface	1
						superstructure	30
	25		120		76		45

Structure 9N-69 = 4,021

Procurement		Transport		Manufacture		Construction	
earth	47	earth	65	masonry	961	walls	104
cobbles	25	cobbles	60	plaster	338	fill	13
tuff	369	tuff	1,881			cobbled surface	1
		plaster	154			plaster surface	3
	441		2,160		1,299		121

Structure 9N-72 = 2,228

Procurement		Transport		Manufacture		Construction	
earth	13	earth	18	masonry	535	walls	58
cobbles	5	cobbles	32	plaster	198	fill	10
tuff	205	tuff	1,048			cobbled surface	6
		plaster	90			plaster surface	10
	223		1,188		733		84

Structure 9N-71 = 1,439

Procurement		Transport		Manufacture		Construction	
earth	5	earth	6	masonry	357	walls	39
cobbles	2	cobbles	9	plaster	119	fill	3
tuff	137	tuff	700			cobbled surface	7
		plaster	54			plaster surface	1
	144		769		476		50

Structure 9N-97 = 3,890

Procurement		Transport		Manufacture		Construction	
earth	14	earth	20	masonry	871	walls	94
cobbles	3	cobbles	22	plaster	439	fill	6
tuff	361	tuff	1,845	cobbles	8	cobbled surface	5
		plaster	200			plaster surface	2
	378		2,087		1,318		107

Structure 9N-92 = 256

Procurement		Transport		Manufacture		Construction	
earth	13	earth	18	cobbles	6	walls	12
cobbles	8	cobbles	47	plaster	53	fill	3
		plaster	24			cobbled surface	6
						plaster surface	1
						superstructure	65
	21		89		59		87

Structure 9N-95 = 39

Procurement		Transport		Manufacture		Construction	
earth	3	earth	4	cobbles	3	walls	3
cobbles	1	cobbles	8			fill	1
						cobbled surface	1
						superstructure	15
	4		12		3		20

Structure 9N-108 = 31

Procurement		Transport		Manufacture		Construction	
earth	1	earth	1	cobbles	1	walls	1
cobbles	1	cobbles	3	plaster	9	superstructure	10
		plaster	4				
	2		8		10		11

Structure 9N-91 = 1,488

Procurement		Transport		Manufacture		Construction	
earth	2	earth	6	masonry	395	walls	53
cobbles	2	cobbles	23	cobbles	10	fill	4
tuff	151	tuff	773	plaster	44	cobbled surface	4
		plaster	20			plaster surface	1
	155		822		449		62

Structure 9M-212 = 127

Procurement		Transport		Manufacture		Construction	
earth	7	earth	9	cobbles	2	walls	4
cobbles	1	cobbles	9	masonry	20	fill	1
tuff	8	tuff	40	plaster	4	cobbled surface	1
		plaster	2			superstructure	19
	16		60		26		25

Structure 9M–213–A = 76

Procurement		Transport		Manufacture		Construction	
earth	5	earth	7	cobbles	1	walls	4
cobbles	2	cobbles	11	masonry	9	cobbled surface	4
tuff	4	tuff	19			superstructure	10
	11		37		10		18

Structure 9M–213–B = 20

Procurement		Transport		Manufacture		Construction	
earth	2	earth	2	cobbles	1	walls	1
		cobbles	2			superstructure	12
	2		4		1		13

Structure 3O–27 = 29

Procurement		Transport		Manufacture		Construction	
earth	2	earth	3	cobbles	2	walls	2
cobbles	1	cobbles	6			cobbled surface	3
						superstructure	10
	3		9		2		15

Structure 3O–28 = 67

Procurement		Transport		Manufacture		Construction	
earth	4	earth	6	cobbles	3	walls	3
cobbles	1	cobbles	11			superstructure	39
	5		17		3		42

Structure 3O–29–1 = 40

Procurement		Transport		Manufacture		Construction	
earth	5	earth	2	cobbles	5	walls	4
cobbles	1	cobbles	8			superstructure	15
	6		10		5		19

Site 7D–6–2 Structure 1 = 32

Procurement		Transport		Manufacture		Construction	
earth	5	earth	6	cobbles	1	walls	3
cobbles	1	cobbles	4			cobbled surface	2
						superstructure	10
	6		10		1		15

Site 7D-6-2 Structure 2 = 71

Procurement		Transport		Manufacture		Construction	
earth	7	earth	10	cobbles	4	walls	4
cobbles	2	cobbles	10			cobbled surface	4
						superstructure	30
	9		20		4		38

Site 7D-6-2 Structure 3 = 21

Procurement		Transport		Manufacture		Construction	
earth	1	earth	2	cobbles	1	walls	1
cobbles	1	cobbles	3			cobbled surface	2
						superstructure	10
	2		5		1		13

Site 7D-3-1 Structure 1 = 37

Procurement		Transport		Manufacture		Construction	
earth	4	earth	5	cobbles	3	walls	3
cobbles	1	cobbles	7			cobbled surface	2
						superstructure	12
	5		12		3		17

Site 7D-3-1 Structure 2 = 23

Procurement		Transport		Manufacture		Construction	
earth	1	earth	2	cobbles	1	walls	1
cobbles	1	cobbles	4			cobbled surface	3
						superstructure	10
	2		6		1		14

Site 11D-11-2 Structure 1 = 42

Procurement		Transport		Manufacture		Construction	
earth	5	earth	7	cobbles	4	walls	5
cobbles	1	cobbles	8			cobbled surface	2
						superstructure	10
	6		15		4		17

Site 11D-11-2 Structure 1-sub = 53

Procurement		Transport		Manufacture		Construction	
earth	7	earth	10	cobbles	4	walls	4
cobbles	2	cobbles	9			cobbled surface	3
						superstructure	14
	9		19		4		21

Costs per Task per Structure

Site 11D–11–2 Structure 2 = 45							
Procurement		*Transport*		*Manufacture*		*Construction*	
earth	6	earth	8	cobbles	4	walls	4
cobbles	1	cobbles	8			cobbled surface	2
						superstructure	12
	7		16		4		18

Appendix B.
Reuse Savings

Reuse savings (expressed in p-d) were generated only in those cases with sufficient evidence of reuse.

Structure 9N-82-C = 2,119

Procurement		Transport		Manufacture	
earth	73	earth	101	masonry	488
cobbles	44	cobbles	269		
tuff	187	tuff	957		
	304		1,327		488

Structure 9N-80 = 356

Procurement		Transport		Manufacture	
earth	17	earth	23	masonry	87
cobbles	4	cobbles	22		
tuff	33	tuff	170		
	54		215		87

Structure 9M-193-B = 96

Procurement		Transport	
earth	13	earth	18
cobbles	4	cobbles	61
	17		79

Structure 9M-197 = 100

Procurement		Transport	
earth	18	earth	24
cobbles	4	cobbles	54
	22		78

Structure 9M-245-B = 56
(all tuff masonry was looted from Structure 9M-196)

Procurement		Transport		Manufacture	
tuff	7	tuff	30	masonry	19

Structure 9N-74-B = 323

Procurement		Transport		Manufacture	
earth	11	earth	15	masonry	81
cobbles	4	cobbles	22		
tuff	31	tuff	159		
	46		196		81

Structure 9N-74-C = 478

Procurement		Transport		Manufacture	
earth	10	earth	13	masonry	147
cobbles	3	cobbles	19		
tuff	57	tuff	229		
	70		261		147

Structure 9N-74-A = 509

Procurement		Transport		Manufacture	
earth	12	earth	17	masonry	135
cobbles	4	cobbles	25		
tuff	52	tuff	264		
	68		306		135

Structure 9N-71 = 56

Procurement		Transport	
earth	11	earth	16
cobbles	4	cobbles	25
	15		41

Structure 9N–91 = 177							
Procurement		*Transport*		*Manufacture*		*Construction*	
earth	5	earth	4	masonry	44	walls	6
cobbles	4	cobbles	10	cobbles	1		
tuff	17	tuff	86				
	26		100		45		6

References

Aaberg, S., and J. Bonsignore
  1975 A Consideration of Time and Labor Expenditure in the Construction
    Process at the Teotihuacan Pyramid of the Sun and the Poverty Point
    Mound. In *Three Papers on Mesoamerican Archaeology,* ed. J. A. Graham and
    R. F. Heizer, pp. 40–78. Contributions of the University of California
    Archaeological Research Facility 24. Berkeley.
Abrams, E. M.
  1984a Systems of Labor Organization in Late Classic Copan, Honduras: The
    Energetics of Construction. Ph.D. diss., Pennsylvania State University,
    University Park.
  1984b Replicative Experimentation at Copan, Honduras: Implications for
    Ancient Economic Specialization. *Journal of New World Archaeology* 6(2):
    39–48.
  1987 Economic Specialization and Construction Personnel in Classic Period
    Copan, Honduras. *American Antiquity* 52(3): 485–499.
  1989 Architecture and Energy: An Evolutionary Perspective. In *Archaeologi-
    cal Method and Theory,* ed. M. Schiffer, 1:47–88. Tucson: University of
    Arizona Press.
Acha, P., and B. Szyfres
  1980 *Zoonoses and Communicable Diseases Common to Man and Animal.* Wash-
    ington, D.C.: Pan American Health Organization.
Adams, R. E. W.
  1970 Suggested Classic Period Occupational Specialization in the Southern
    Maya Lowlands. In *Monographs and Papers in Maya Archaeology,* ed. W. Bul-
    lard. Papers of the Peabody Museum of Archaeology and Ethnology 61.
    Cambridge, Mass.
  1977 Rio Bec Archaeology and the Rise of Maya Civilization. In *The Origins*

of Maya Civilization, ed. R. E. W. Adams, pp. 77–99. Albuquerque: University of New Mexico Press.

Adams, R. E. W., and W. D. Smith

1981   Feudal Models for Classic Maya Civilization. In *Lowland Maya Settlement Patterns,* ed. W. Ashmore, pp. 335–349. Albuquerque: University of New Mexico Press.

Adams, R. N.

1975   *Energy and Structure.* Austin: University of Texas Press.

Aldenderfer, M., L. Kimball, and A. Sievert

1989   Microwear Analysis in the Maya Lowlands: The Use of Functional Data in a Complex-Society Setting. *Journal of Field Archaeology* 16: 47–60.

Andrews, E. W., IV, and I. Rovner

1973   Archaeological Evidence on Social Stratification and Commerce in the Northern Maya Lowlands: Two Masons' Tool Kits from Muna and Dzibilchaltun, Yucatan. In *Archaeological Investigations on the Yucatan Peninsula,* pp. 81–102. Middle American Research Institute Publication 31. New Orleans.

Andrews, E. W., V, and B. Fash

1992   Continuity and Change in a Royal Maya Residential Complex at Copan. *Ancient Mesoamerica* 3: 63–88.

Andrews, G.

1975   *Maya Cities: Placemaking and Urbanism.* Norman: University of Oklahoma Press.

Arnold, J., and A. Ford

1980   A Statistical Examination of Settlement Patterns at Tikal, Guatemala. *American Antiquity* 45(4): 713–726.

Ashmore, W.

1981   Some Issues of Method and Theory in Lowland Maya Settlement Archaeology. In *Lowland Maya Settlement Patterns,* ed. W. Ashmore, pp. 37–69. Albuquerque: University of New Mexico Press.

1986   Peten Cosmology in the Maya Southeast: An Analysis of Architecture and Settlement Patterns. In *The Southeast Maya Periphery,* ed. P. Urban and E. Schortman, pp. 35–49. Austin: University of Texas Press.

1988   Household and Community at Classic Quirigua. In *Household and Community in the Mesoamerican Past,* ed. R. Wilk and W. Ashmore, pp. 153–170. Albuquerque: University of New Mexico Press.

1991   Site-Planning Principles and Concepts of Directionality among the Ancient Maya. *Latin American Antiquity* 2(3): 199–226.

Ashmore, W., and G. Willey

1981   A Historical Introduction to the Study of Lowland Maya Settlement Patterns. In *Lowland Maya Settlement Patterns,* ed. W. Ashmore, pp. 3–18. Albuquerque: University of New Mexico Press.

Baudez, C.

1983   (Ed.) *Introducción a la arqueología de Copán, Honduras.* 3 vols. Tegucigalpa: Secretaría de Estado en el Despacho de Cultura y Turismo.

Becker, M.

1973 Archaeological Evidence for Occupational Specialization among the Classic Period Maya at Tikal, Guatemala. *American Antiquity* 38: 396–406.

1983 Excavaciones en el Corte de la Acropolis. In *Introducción a la arqueología de Copán, Honduras,* ed. C. Baudez, 2: 349–379. Tegucigalpa: Secretaría de Estado en el Despacho de Cultura y Turismo.

Bennett, J.

1968 Reciprocal Economic Exchanges among North American Agricultural Operators. *American Antiquity* 24(3): 276–309.

Bennett, W. C.

1963 A Cross-Cultural Survey of South American Indian Tribes: Architecture and Engineering-habitations. In *Handbook of South American Indians,* ed. J. Steward, 5: 1–20. New York: Cooper Square.

Bierbrier, M.

1982 *The Tomb-Builders of the Pharaohs.* London: British Museum.

Binford, L.

1989 Science to Seance, or Processual to "Post-processual" Archaeology. In *Debating Archaeology,* by L. Binford, pp. 27–40. New York: Academic Press.

Boas, F.

1964 *The Central Eskimo.* Lincoln: University of Nebraska Press.

Bohanan, P.

1959 Some Principles of Exchange and Investment among the Tiv. *American Anthropologist* 57: 60–70.

Bonwick, J.

1967 *Daily Life and Origin of the Tasmanians.* London: Sampson, Low, Son, and Marston. Originally published in 1870.

Bullard, W.

1960 Maya Settlement Patterns in Northeastern Peten, Guatemala. *American Antiquity* 25: 355–372.

Callahan, E. H.

1981 Pamunkey Housebuilding: An Experimental Study of Late Woodland Construction Technology in the Powhatan Confederacy. Ph.D. diss., Catholic University, Washington, D.C.

Campbell, D.

1965 Variation and Selective Retention in Sociocultural Evolution. In *Social Change in Developing Areas: A Reinterpretation of Evolutionary Theory,* ed. H. R. Barringer, G. I. Blanksten, and R. W. Mack, pp. 19–49. Cambridge, Mass.: Schenkman.

Carmean, K.

1991 Architectural Labor Investment and Social Stratification at Sayil, Yucatan, Mexico. *Latin American Antiquity* 2(2): 151–165.

Chapple, E., and S. Coon

1942 *Principles of Anthropology.* New York: Holt and Co.

Chase, D., and A. Chase.
   1992 (Eds.) *Mesoamerican Elites: An Archaeological Assessment.* Norman: University of Oklahoma Press.
Chase, D., A. Chase, and W. Haviland
   1990 The Classic Maya City: Reconsidering the "Mesoamerican Urban Tradition." *American Anthropologist* 92(2): 499–506.
Cheek, C.
   1983 Excavaciones en la Plaza Principál. In *Introducción a la arqueología de Copán, Honduras,* ed. C. Baudez, 2: 191–289. Tegucigalpa: Secretaría de Estado en el Despacho de Cultura y Turismos.
   1986 Construction Activity as a Measurement of Change at Copan, Honduras. In *The Southeast Maya Periphery,* ed. P. Urban and E. Schortman, pp. 50–71. Austin: University of Texas Press.
Cheek, C., and M. Spink
   1986 Excavaciones en el Grupo 3, Estructura 223 (Operación VII). In *Excavaciones en el área urbana de Copán,* ed. W. Sanders, 1: 27–154. Tegucigalpa: Secretaría de Cultura y Turismo, Instituto Hondureño de Antropología e Historia.
Childe, V. G.
   1950 The Urban Revolution. *Town Planning Review* 21: 3–17.
Coe, M.
   1957 The Khmer Settlement Pattern: A Possible Analogy with That of the Maya. *American Antiquity* 22: 409–410.
Cohodas, M.
   1976 The Identification of Workshops, Schools, and Hands at Yaxchilan, a Classic Maya Site in Mexico. *International Congress of Americanists* 37: 301–313.
Coimbra, C. E. A.
   1988 Human Settlements, Demographic Pattern, and Epidemiology in Lowland Amazonia: The Case of Chagas's Disease. *American Anthropologist* 90(1): 82–97.
Costin, C. L.
   1991 Craft Specialization: Issues in Defining, Documenting, and Explaining the Organization of Production. In *Archaeological Method and Theory,* ed. M. Schiffer, 3: 1–56. Tucson: University of Arizona Press.
Coy, M.
   1989 (Ed.) *Apprenticeships.* Albany: SUNY Press.
Culbert, T. P.
   1977 Early Maya Development at Tikal, Guatemala. In *The Origins of Maya Civilization,* ed. R. E. W. Adams, pp. 27–43. Albuquerque: University of New Mexico Press.
Demarest, A.
   1991 Ideology in Ancient Maya Cultural Evolution: The Dynamics of Galactic Polities. In *Ideology and the Evolution of Precolumbian Civilization,* ed. A. Demarest and G. Conrad, pp. 135–157. Albuquerque: University of New Mexico Press.

Diamanti, M.

 1991 Domestic Organization at Copan: Reconstruction of Elite Maya House-holds through Ethnographic Models. Ph.D. diss., Pennsylvania State University, University Park.

Earle, T.

 1981 Comment on "Evolution of Specialized Pottery: A Trial Model," by P. Rice. *Current Anthropology* 22: 230–231.

 1991 Property Rights and the Evolution of Chiefdoms. In *Chiefdoms: Power, Economy and Ideology,* ed. T. Earle, pp. 71–99. Cambridge: Cambridge University Press.

Eaton, J.

 1991 Tools of Ancient Maya Builders. In *Maya Stone Tools: Selected Papers from the Second Maya Lithic Conference,* ed. T. Hester and H. Shafer, pp. 219–228. Monographs in World Archaeology, no. 1. Madison: Prehistory Press.

Economic Commission for Asia and the Far East (ECAFE)

 1957 Manual Labor and Its More Effective Use in Competition with Machines for Earthwork in the ESCAFE Region. United Nations E/CN.11/conf. 3/ L.I. Manila, Philippines.

Erasmus, C.

 1956 Cultural Structure and Process: The Occurrence and Disappearance of Reciprocal Farm Labor. *Southwestern Journal of Anthropology* 12: 444–471.

 1965 Monument Building: Some Field Experiments. *Southwestern Journal of Anthropology* 21: 277–301.

Fash, B., W. Fash, S. Lane, R. Larios, L. Schele, J. Stomper, and D. Stuart

 1992 Investigations of a Classic Maya Council House at Copan, Honduras. *Journal of Field Archaeology* 19(4): 419–442.

Fash, W.

 1983 Maya State Formation: A Case Study and Its Implications. Ph.D. diss., Harvard University.

 1989 The Sculptural Facade of Structure 9N-82: Content, Form, and Significance. In *The House of the Bacabs, Copan, Honduras,* ed. D. Webster, pp. 41–72. Washington, D.C.: Dumbarton Oaks.

 1991a *Scribes, Warriors and Kings.* London: Thames and Hudson.

 1991b Lineage Patrons and Ancestor Worship among the Classic Maya Nobility: The Case of Copan Structure 9N-82. In *Sixth Palenque Round Table, 1986,* ed. V. Fields, pp. 68–80. Norman: University of Oklahoma Press.

Fash, W., and R. Sharer

 1991 Sociopolitical Developments and Methodological Issues at Copan, Honduras: A Conjunctive Perspective. *Latin American Antiquity* 2: 166–187.

Fash, W., and D. Stuart

 1991 Dynastic History and Cultural Evolution at Copan, Honduras. In *Classic Maya Political History,* ed. T. Patrick Culbert, pp. 147–179. Cambridge: Cambridge University Press.

Fash, W., R. Williamson, C. R. Larios, and J. Palka
   1992   The Hieroglyphic Stairway and Its Ancestors: Investigations of Copan
          Structure 10L-26. *Ancient Mesoamerica* 3(1): 105–115.
Firth, R.
   1965   *Primitive Polynesian Economy.* New York: W. W. Norton.
Fitch, J., and D. Branch
   1960   Primitive Architecture and Climate. *Scientific American* 203(6): 134–145.
Folan, W., E. Kintz, L. Fletcher, and B. Hyde
   1982   An Examination of Settlement Patterns at Coba, Quintana Roo, Mex-
          ico, and Tikal, Guatemala: A Reply to Arnold and Ford. *American Antiq-
          uity* 47(2): 430–435.
Ford, A.
   1991   Economic Variation of Ancient Maya Residential Settlement in the Up-
          per Belize River Area. *Ancient Mesoamerica* 2(1): 35–46.
Forde, C. D.
   1963   *Habitat, Economy and Society.* New York: E. P. Dutton.
Freidel, D., and L. Schele
   1989   Dead Kings and Living Temples: Dedication and Termination Rituals
          among the Ancient Maya. In *Word and Image in Maya Culture,* ed. W. Hanks
          and D. Rice, pp. 233–243. Salt Lake City: University of Utah Press.
Freter, A.
   1988   The Classic Maya Collapse at Copan, Honduras: A Regional Settlement
          Perspective. Ph.D. diss. Pennsylvania State University, University Park.
   1991   A Reconstruction of the Late Classic Rural Ceramic Production Sys-
          tem in the Copan Valley, Honduras. Paper presented at the Fifty-sixth An-
          nual Meeting of the Society for American Archaeology, New Orleans.
   1992   Chronological Research at Copan: Methods and Implications. *Ancient
          Mesoamerica* 3: 117–134.
Fried, M.
   1967   *The Evolution of Political Society.* New York: Random House.
Gifford, E.
   1929   *Tongan Society.* B. P. Bishop Museum Bulletin 61. Honolulu.
Givoni, B.
   1969   *Man, Climate and Architecture.* New York: Elsevier.
Goldman, I.
   1970   *Ancient Polynesian Society.* Chicago: University of Chicago Press.
Gonlin, N.
   1985   The Architectural Variation of Two Small Sites in the Copan Valley,
          Honduras: A Rural/Urban Dichotomy? Master's thesis, Pennsylvania State
          University, University Park.
   1993   *Rural Household Archaeology at Copan, Honduras.* Ph.D. diss., Pennsyl-
          vania State University, University Park.
Goody, E.
   1989   Learning, Apprenticeship and the Division of Labor. In *Apprenticeship,*
          ed. M. Coy, pp. 233–256. Albany: SUNY Press.

Gordon, G. B.

1896 *Prehistoric Ruins of Copan, Honduras.* Memoirs of the Peabody Museum of Archaeology and Ethnology, vol. 1, no. 1. Cambridge, Mass.: Harvard University.

1902 *The Hieroglyphic Stairway, Ruins of Copan.* Memoirs of the Peabody Museum of Archaeology and Ethnology, vol. 1, no. 6. Cambridge, Mass.: Harvard University.

Gregory, C. A., and J. C. Altman

1989 *Observing the Economy.* London: Routledge.

Halperin, R.

1990 *The Livelihood of Kin.* Austin: University of Texas Press.

Hammond, N.

1977 Ex Oriente Lux: A View from Belize. In *The Origins of Maya Civilization,* ed. R. E. W. Adams, pp. 45–76. Albuquerque: University of New Mexico Press.

1991a (Ed.) *Cuello: An Early Maya Community in Belize.* Cambridge: Cambridge University Press.

1991b Inside the Black Box: Defining Maya Polity. In *Classic Maya Political History,* ed. T. P. Culbert, pp. 253–284. New York: Cambridge University Press.

Hammond, N., and J. Gerhardt

1990 Early Maya Architectural Innovation at Cuello, Belize. *World Archaeology* 21: 461–481.

Handy, E., S. Craighill, and W. C. Handy

1924 *Samoan House Building, Cooking, and Tatooing.* B. P. Bishop Museum Bulletin 15. Honolulu.

Harris, M.

1968 *The Rise of Anthropological Theory.* New York: Crowell.

1979 *Cultural Materialism.* New York: Random House.

Haviland, W.

1974 Occupational Specialization at Tikal, Guatemala: Stoneworking—Monument carving. *American Antiquity* 39: 494–496.

1981 Dower Houses and Minor Centers at Tikal, Guatemala: An Investigation into the Identification of Valid Units in Settlement Hierarchies. In *Lowland Maya Settlement Patterns,* ed. W. Ashmore, pp. 89–117. Albuquerque: University of New Mexico Press.

1985 *Excavations in Small Residential Groups of Tikal: Groups 4F-1 and 4F-2.* Tikal Report 19, University Museum Monograph 58. Philadelphia: The University Museum, University of Pennsylvania.

1988 Musical Hammocks at Tikal: Problems with Reconstructing Household Composition. In *Household and Community in the Mesoamerican Past,* ed. R. Wilk and W. Ashmore, pp. 135–152. Albuquerque: University of New Mexico Press.

Haviland, W., and H. Moholy-Nagy

1992 Distinguishing the High and Mighty from the Hoi Polloi at Tikal, Guatemala. In *Mesoamerican Elites: An Archaeological Assessment,* ed. D. Chase and A. Chase, pp. 50–60. Norman: University of Oklahoma Press.

Helms, M.

   1979   *Ancient Panama.* Austin: University of Texas Press.

Hendon, J.

   1991   Status and Power in Classic Maya Society: An Archaeological Study. *American Anthropologist* 93(4): 894–918.

Henry, T.

   1928   *Ancient Tahiti.* B. P. Bishop Museum Bulletin 48. Honolulu.

Herskovits, M.

   1938   *Dahomey, An Ancient West African Kingdom.* Vol. 1. New York: Augustin.

Hillier, B., and J. Hanson

   1984   *The Social Logic of Space.* Cambridge: Cambridge University Press.

Hiroa, T.

   1934   *Mangaian Society.* B. P. Bishop Museum Bulletin 122. Honolulu.

Hirth, K.

   1984   (Ed.)   *Trade and Exchange in Early Mesoamerica.* Albuquerque: University of New Mexico Press.

Hogbin, I.

   1914   *A Guadalcanal Society: The Kaoka Speaks.* New York: Holt, Rinehart and Winston.

Hohmann, H., and A. Vogrin

   1982   *Die Architektur von Copan (Honduras).* Graz, Austria: Akademische Druck- und Verlagsanstalt.

Holmberg, A.

   1969   *Nomads of the Long Bow.* New York: Natural History Press.

Hosler, D. H., J. A. Sabloff, and D. Runge.

   1977   Simulation Model Development: A Case Study of the Classic Maya Collapse. In *Social Process in Maya Prehistory,* ed. N. Hammond, pp. 553–590. London: Academic Press.

Hyman, D.

   1970   *Precolumbian Cements: A Study of the Calcareous Cements in Prehispanic Mesoamerican Building Construction.* Baltimore: Johns Hopkins University Press.

Kaplan, D.

   1963   Men, Monuments, and Political Systems. *Southwestern Journal of Anthropology* 19: 397–410.

Kent, S.

   1990   (Ed.)   *Domestic Architecture and the Use of Space.* Cambridge: Cambridge University Press.

Kidder, A. V.

   1950   Introduction. In *Uaxactun, Guatemala: Excavations of 1931–1937,* by A. Ledyard Smith. Carnegie Institution of Washington Publication 588. Washington, D.C.

Knuffel, W.
  1973   *The Construction of the Bantu Grass Hut*. Graz, Austria: Akademische Druck- und Verlagsanstalt.
Kolb, M.
  1991   *Social Power, Chiefly Authority, and Ceremonial Architecture, in an Island Polity, Maui, Hawaii*. Ph.D. diss., University of California, Los Angeles.
Koth, M., J. Silva, and A. Dietz
  1965   *Housing in Latin America*. Cambridge, Mass.: MIT Press.
Kurjack, E.
  1974   *Prehistoric Lowland Maya Community and Social Organization*. Middle American Research Institute Publication 38. New Orleans.
Lange, F., and C. Ryberg
  1972   Abandonment and Post-abandonment Behavior at a Rural Central American House Site. *American Antiquity* 37(3): 419–432.
Lawrence, D., and S. Low
  1990   The Built Environment and Spatial Form. *Annual Review of Anthropology* 19: 453–505.
Lee, R.
  1979   *The !Kung San*. Cambridge: Cambridge University Press.
Lekson, S.
  1984   *Great Pueblo Architecture of Chaco Canyon*. Publications in Archaeology 18B, Chaco Canyon Studies. Albuquerque: National Park Service.
Lentz, D.
  1991   Maya Diets of the Rich and Poor: Paleoethnobotanical Evidence from Copan. *Latin American Antiquity* 2: 269–287.
Leventhal, R.
  1979   *Settlement Patterns at Copan, Honduras*. Ph.D. diss., Harvard University.
Lewenstein, S.
  1987   *Stone Tool Use at Cerros*. Austin: University of Texas Press.
Loewe, M.
  1968   *Everyday Life in Early Imperial China*. New York: G. P. Putnam.
Longyear, J.
  1952   *Copan Ceramics: A Study of Southeastern Maya Pottery*. Carnegie Institution of Washington Publication 597. Washington, D.C.
Loten, S.
  1990   Monumentality: Power and Dwellings in the Maya Lowlands. Paper presented at the Eighty-ninth Annual Meeting of the American Anthropological Association, New Orleans.
Loten, S., and D. Pendergast
  1984   *A Lexicon for Maya Architecture*. Royal Ontario Museum Archaeology Monograph 8. Toronto.
MacNeish, R., S. J. Wilkerson, and A. Nelken-Terner
  1980   *First Annual Report of the Belize Archaic Archaeological Reconnaissance*. Andover, Mass.: Peabody Foundation for Archaeology.

Mahoney, W.
  1981 *Repair and Remodeling Cost Data.* Kingston, Mass.: Robert Snow
  Means.
Malinowski, B.
  1960 *A Scientific Theory of Culture and Other Essays.* New York: Oxford University Press.
Mallory, J.
  1984 *Late Classic Maya Economic Specialization: Evidence from the Copan Obsidian Assemblage.* Ph.D. diss., Pennsylvania State University.
Matheny, R.
  1980 *El Mirador, Peten, Guatemala: An Interim Report.* Papers of the New World Archaeological Foundation, no. 45. Provo, Utah: Brigham Young University.
Maudslay, A.
  1889–1902 Archaeology. In *Biologia Centrali-Americana.* 5 vols. London: Porter and Dulau.
McAnany, P., and B. Issac
  1989 (Eds.) Prehistoric Maya Economies of Belize. *Research in Economic Anthropology,* Supplement no. 4.
McGuire, R.
  1983 Breaking Down Cultural Complexity: Inequality and Heterogeneity. In *Advances in Archaeological Method and Theory,* ed. M. Schiffer, 6: 91–142. New York: Academic Press.
McGuire, R., and M. Schiffer
  1983 A Theory of Architectural Design. *Journal of Anthropological Archaeology* 2: 227–303.
Mendelssohn, K.
  1974 *The Riddle of the Pyramids.* New York: Praeger.
Mills, C. W.
  1956 *The Power Elite.* London: Oxford University Press.
Morgan, L. H.
  1881 *Houses and House-life of the American Aborigines.* Chicago: University of Chicago Press.
Morley, S. G.
  1920 *The Inscriptions of Copan.* Carnegie Institution of Washington Publication 437. Washington, D.C.
  1946 *The Ancient Maya.* Stanford: Stanford University Press.
Morris, E. H., J. Charlot, and A. A. Morris
  1931 *The Temple of the Warriors at Chichen Itza, Yucatan.* 2 vols. Carnegie Institution of Washington Publication 406. Washington, D.C.
Nadel, S. F.
  1942 *A Black Byzantium.* London: Oxford University Press.
O'Brien, P., and H. Christiansen
  1986 An Ancient Maya Measurement System. *American Antiquity* 5(1): 136–151.

Odum, H. T.
1971 *Environment, Power, and Society.* New York: Wiley.

Oliver, P.
1987 *Dwellings: The House across the World.* Austin: University of Texas Press.

Peebles, C., and S. Kus
1977 Some Archaeological Correlates of Ranked Societies. *American Antiquity* 42: 421–448.

Polanyi, K.
1957 The Economy as Instituted Process. In *Trade and Market in the Early Empires,* ed. K. Polanyi, C. Arensberg, and H. Pearson, pp. 243–270. New York: Free Press.

Pollock, H. E. D.
1965 Architecture of the Maya Lowlands. In *Handbook of Middle American Indians,* ed. G. Willey, 2: 378–440. Austin: University of Texas Press.

Pozorski, T.
1980 The Early Horizon Site of Huaca de los Reyes: Societal Implications. *American Antiquity* 45: 100–110.

Price, B.
1982 Cultural Materialism: A Theoretical Review. *American Antiquity* 47(4): 709–741.
1984 Competition, Productive Intensification, and Ranked Society: Speculation from Evolutionary Theory. In *Warfare, Culture, and Environment,* ed. B. Ferguson, pp. 209–240. New York: Academic Press.

Proskouriakoff, T.
1946 *An Album of Maya Architecture.* Carnegie Institution of Washington Publication 558. Washington, D.C.

Pyburn, K. A.
1990 Settlement Patterns at Nohmul: Preliminary Results of Four Excavation Seasons. In *Precolumbian Population History in the Maya Lowlands,* ed. T. P. Culbert and D. S. Rice, pp. 183–197. Albuquerque: University of New Mexico Press.

Rapoport, A.
1969 *House Form and Culture.* Englewood Cliffs, N.J.: Prentice-Hall.

Redfield, R., and A. Villa R.
1964 *Chan Kom: A Maya Village.* Chicago: University of Chicago Press.

Reed, N., J. Bennett, and J. Porter
1968 Solid Core Drilling of Monks Mound: Technique and Findings. *American Antiquity* 33: 137–148.

Renfrew, C.
1973 Monuments, Mobilization and Social Organization in Neolithic Wessex. In *The Explanation of Culture Change: Models in Prehistory,* ed. C. Renfrew, pp. 539–558. London: Duckworth.
1983 The Social Archaeology of Megalithic Monuments. *Scientific American* 249(5): 152–163.

Rice, P.

1981   Evolution of Specialized Pottery Production: A Trial Model. *Current Anthropology* 22(3): 219–240.

Rindos, D.

1984   *The Origins of Agriculture: An Evolutionary Perspective.* New York: Academic Press.

Ringle, W., and E. W. Andrews V

1988   Formative Residences at Komchen, Yucatan, Mexico. In *Household and Community in the Mesoamerican Past,* ed. R. Wilk and W. Ashmore, pp. 171–198. Albuquerque: University of New Mexico Press.

Robbins, M.

1966   House Types and Settlement Patterns: An Application of Ethnology to Archaeological Interpretation. *Minnesota Archaeologist* 28(1): 3–26.

Roys, L.

1934   *The Engineering Knowledge of the Maya.* Carnegie Institution of Washington Publication 436, no. 6, pp. 27–105. Washington, D.C.

Rue, D.

1987   Early Agricultural and Early Postclassic Occupation in Western Honduras. *Nature* 326(6110): 285–286.

Sahlins, M.

1972   *Stone Age Economics.* Chicago: Aldine.

Sanders, W.

1976   The Fon of Bafut and the Classic Maya. *Papers of the XLII International Congress of Americanists* 8: 389–399.

1981   Classic Maya Settlement Patterns and Ethnographic Analogy. In *Lowland Maya Settlement Patterns,* ed. W. Ashmore, pp. 351–369. Albuquerque: University of New Mexico Press.

1986a   (Ed.) *Excavaciones en el área urbana de Copán.* Vol. 1. Tegucigalpa: Secretaría de Cultura y Turismo. Instituto Hondureño de Antropología e Historia.

1986b   Introducción. In *Excavaciones en el área urbana de Copán,* ed. W. Sanders, 1: 9–25. Tegucigalpa: Secretaría de Cultura y Turismo, Instituto Hondureño de Antropología e Historia.

1989   Household, Lineage and the State in 8th-Century Copan. In *House of the Bacabs, Copan: A Study of the Iconography, Epigraphy and Social Context of a Maya Elite Structure,* ed. D. Webster, pp. 89–105. Washington, D.C.: Dumbarton Oaks.

1990   (Ed.) *Excavaciones en el área urbana de Copán.* Vol. 2. Tegucigalpa: Secretaría de Cultura y Turismo, Instituto Hondureño de Antropología e Historia.

1992   Ranking and Stratification in Prehispanic Mesoamerica. In *Mesoamerican Elites: An Archaeological Assessment,* ed. D. Chase and A. Chase, pp. 278–291. Norman: University of Oklahoma Press.

Sanders, W., and B. Price

1968   *Mesoamerica: The Evolution of a Civilization.* New York: Random House.

Sanderson, S.

1990   *Social Evolutionism.* Cambridge, Mass.: Basil Blackwell.

Satterthwaite, L.

1954   *Unclassified Buildings and Substructures.* Part 4 of *Piedras Negras Archaeology: Architecture.* Philadelphia: The University Museum, University of Pennsylvania.

Scarborough, V., and G. Gallopin

1991   A Water Storage Adaptation in the Maya Lowlands. *Science* 251: 658–662.

Schele, L.

1985   Color on Classic Architecture and Monumental Sculpture of the Southern Maya Lowlands. In *Painted Architecture and Polychrome Monumental Sculpture in Mesoamerica,* ed. E. Boone, pp. 31–49. Washington, D.C.: Dumbarton Oaks.

1989   The Copan Lectures. Transcript of lectures at the Thirteenth Maya Hieroglyphic Workshop, Austin, Texas.

Schele, L., and M. Miller

1986   *The Blood of Kings.* Fort Worth, Tex.: Kimbell Art Museum.

Service, E.

1962   *Primitive Social Organization.* New York: Random House.

Shafer, H., and T. Hester

1986   Maya Tool Craft Specialization and Production at Colha, Belize: A Reply to Mallory. *American Antiquity* 51(1): 158–166.

Sharer, R.

1991   Diversity and Continuity in Maya Civilization: Quirigua as a Case Study. In *Classic Maya Political History,* ed. T. P. Culbert, pp. 180–198. Albuquerque: University of New Mexico Press.

Sharer, R., J. Miller, and L. Traxler

1992   Evolution of Classic Period Architecture in the Eastern Acropolis, Copan, Honduras: A Progress Report. *Ancient Mesoamerica* 3: 145–160.

Sheehy, J.

1991   Structure and Change in a Late Classic Maya Domestic Group at Copan, Honduras. *Ancient Mesoamerica* 2(1): 1–19.

Sheets, P.

1992   *The Ceren Site.* Orlando: Holt, Rinehart and Winston.

Shimkin, D.

1973   Models for the Downfall: Some Ecological and Culture-Historical Considerations. In *The Classic Maya Collapse,* ed. T. P. Culbert, pp. 269–299. Albuquerque: University of New Mexico Press.

Smith, A. L.

1950   *Uaxactun, Guatemala: Excavations of 1931–1937.* Carnegie Institution of Washington Publication 588. Washington, D.C.

Southall, A.

1991   The Segmentary State: From the Imaginary to the Material Means of Production. In *Early State Economics,* ed. H. Claessen and P. van de Velde, pp. 75–96. New Brunswick, N.J.: Transaction Publishers.

Spink, M.

1983   *Metates as Socioeconomic Indicators during the Classic Period at Copan, Honduras.* Ph.D. diss., Pennsylvania State University, University Park.

Startin, D. W. A.

1982   Prehistoric Earthmoving. In *Settlement Patterns in the Oxford Region: Excavations at the Abingdon Causewayed Enclosure and Other Sites,* ed. H. J. Case and A. W. R. Whittle, pp. 153–161. Council of British Archaeology and Dept. of Antiquities, Ashmolean Museum Research Report 44. Oxford.

Stephens, J. L.

1841   *Incidents of Travel in Central America, Chiapas and Yucatan.* Vol. 1. New York: Dover.

Steward, J.

1955   *Theory of Culture Change.* Urbana: University of Illinois.

Storey, G.

1992   *Preindustrial Urban Demography: The Ancient Roman Evidence.* Ph.D. diss., Pennsylvania State University, University Park.

Storey, R.

1986   Entierros y clase social en Copán, Honduras: Aspectos biológicos. *Yaxkin* 9: 55–61.

Swanson, H.

1989   *Medieval Artisans.* New York: Basil Blackwell.

Thompson, E. H.

1892   The Ancient Structures of Yucatan not Communal Dwellings. *Proceedings of the American Antiquarian Society,* n.s. 8: 262–269.

Thompson, J. E. S.

1954   *The Rise and Fall of Maya Civilization.* Norman: University of Oklahoma Press.

Totten, G.

1926   *Maya Architecture.* Washington, D.C.: Maya Press.

Tourtellot, G.

1988a   *Excavations at Seibal: Peripheral Survey and Excavations.* Memoirs of the Peabody Museum of American Archaeology and Ethnology, no. 16. Cambridge, Mass.: Harvard University.

1988b   Developmental Cycles of Households and Houses at Seibal. In *Household and Community in the Mesoamerican Past,* ed. R. Wilk and W. Ashmore, pp. 97–120. Albuquerque: University of New Mexico Press.

Tourtellot, G., J. Sabloff, and K. Carmean

1992   Will the Real Elites Please Stand Up? An Archaeological Assessment of Maya Elite Behavior. In *Mesoamerican Elites: An Archaeological Assessment,* ed. D. Chase and A. Chase, pp. 80–98. Norman: University of Oklahoma Press.

Tozzer, A. M.

1941   *Landa's Relación de las cosas de Yucatan.* Papers of the Peabody Museum of American Archaeology and Ethnology, vol. 18. Cambridge, Mass.: Harvard University.

Trigger, B.

1990 Monumental Architecture: A Thermodynamic Explanation of Symbolic Behaviour. *World Archaeology* 22(2): 119–132.

Trik, A.

1939 *Temple XXII at Copan.* Contributions to American Anthropology and History, vol. 5, no. 27, Washington, D.C.: Carnegie Institution of Washington.

Turner, B. L., II, W. Johnson, G. Mahood, F. Wiseman, B. L. Turner, and J. Poole

1983 Habitat y agricultura en la región de Copán. In *Introducción a la arqueología de Copán,* ed. C. Baudez, 1: 35–142. Tegucigalpa: Secretaría de Cultura y Turismo, Instituto Hondureño de Antropología e Historia.

Turner, E. S., N. I. Turner, and R. E. W. Adams

1981 Volumetric Assessment, Rank Ordering, and Maya Civic Centers. In *Lowland Maya Settlement Patterns,* ed. W. Ashmore, pp. 71–88. Albuquerque: University of New Mexico Press.

Udy, S.

1959 *The Organization of Work.* New Haven: Human Relations Area Files Press.

Valdez, F., and D. Potter

1991 Chert Debitage from the Harvard Copan Excavations: Descriptions and Comments. In *Maya Stone Tools: Selected Papers from the Second Maya Lithic Conference,* ed. T. Hester and H. Shafer, pp. 203–206. Monographs in World Archaeology, no. 1. Madison: Prehistory Press.

Vlcek, D., and W. Fash

1986 Survey in the Outlying Areas of the Copan Region, and the Copan-Quirigua "Connection." In *The Southeast Maya Periphery,* ed. P. Urban and E. Schortman, pp. 102–113. Austin: University of Texas Press.

Vogt, E.

1969 *Zinacantan.* Cambridge, Mass.: Belknap Press.

Watson, P. J.

1978 Architectural Differentiation in Some Near Eastern Communities, Prehistoric and Contemporary. In *Social Archaeology: Beyond Subsistence and Dating,* ed. C. Redman, M. Berman, E. Curtin, W. Langhorne, Jr., N. Vergassi, and J. Wanser, pp. 131–158. New York: Academic Press.

1986 Archaeological Interpretation, 1985. In *American Archaeology Past and Future,* ed. D. Meltzer, D. Fowler, and J. Sabloff, pp. 439–457. Washington, D.C.: Smithsonian Institution Press.

Watson, P. J., S. LeBlanc, and C. Redman

1984 *Archaeological Explanation: The Scientific Method in Archaeology.* New York: Columbia University Press.

Wauchope, R.

1934 House Mounds at Uaxactun, Guatemala. Carnegie Institution of Washington Publication 436. *Contributions to American Anthropology and History,* no. 7, pp. 107–171. Washington, D.C.

1938 *Modern Maya Houses: A Study of Their Archaeological Significance.* Carnegie Institution of Washington Publication 502. Washington, D.C.

Way, A.
1981 Diseases of Latin America. In *Biocultural Aspects of Disease,* ed. H. Rothchild, pp. 253–291. New York: Academic Press.

Webster, D.
1976 On Theocracies. *American Anthropologist* 78(4): 812–828.
1977 Warfare and the Evolution of Maya Civilization. In *The Origins of Maya Civilization,* ed. R. E. W. Adams, pp. 335–372. Albuquerque: University of New Mexico Press.
1981 Egregious Energetics. *American Antiquity* 46(4): 919–922.
1985 Surplus, Labor and Stress in Late Classic Maya Society. *Journal of Anthropological Research* 41(4): 375–399.
1989 (Ed.) *The House of the Bacabs, Copan, Honduras.* Washington, D.C.: Dumbarton Oaks.
1992 Maya Elites: The Perspective from Copan. In *Mesoamerican Elites: An Archaeological Assessment,* ed. D. Chase and A. Chase, pp. 135–156. Norman: University of Oklahoma Press.

Webster, D., and E. Abrams
1986 An Elite Compound at Copan, Honduras. *Journal of Field Archaeology* 10: 285–296.

Webster, D., W. Fash, and E. Abrams
1986 Excavaciones en el Conjunto 9N-8, Patio A (Operación VIII). In *Excavaciones en el área urbana de Copán,* ed. W. Sanders, 1: 155–317. Tegucigalpa: Secretaría de Cultura y Turismo, Instituto Hondureño de Antropología e Historia.

Webster, D., and A. Freter
1990a Settlement History and the Classic Collapse at Copan: A Redefined Chronological Perspective. *Latin American Antiquity* 1(1): 66–85.
1990b The Demography of Late Classic Copan. In *Precolumbian Population History in the Maya Lowlands,* ed. T. P. Culbert and D. Rice, pp. 37–61. Albuquerque: University of New Mexico Press.

Webster, D., and N. Gonlin
1988 Household Remains of the Humblest Maya. *Journal of Field Archaeology* 15(2): 169–190.

Webster, D., W. Sanders, and P. van Rossum
1992 A Simulation of Copan Population History and Its Implications. *Ancient Mesoamerica* 3: 185–197.

Whiting, J., and B. Ayres
1968 Inferences from the Shape of Dwellings. In *Settlement Archaeology,* ed. K. C. Chang, pp. 117–133. Palo Alto: National Press.

Whitlaw, J., and B. Chaniotis
1978 Palm Trees and Chagas' Disease in Panama. *American Journal of Tropical Medicine and Hygiene* 27(5): 873–881.

Widmer, R.
1993 Excavaciones en el Conjunto 9N-8, Patio H (Operación XXII). In

Proyecto Arqueológico Copán Segunda Fase: Excavaciones en el área urbana de Copán, vol. 5, ed. W. Sanders. Tegucigalpa: Secretaría de Cultura y Turismo, Instituto Hondureño de Antropología e Historia.

Wilk, R.
  1983   Little House in the Jungle: The Causes of Variation in House Size among Modern Maya. *Journal of Anthropological Archaeology* 2: 99–116.
  1988   Maya Household Organization: Evidence and Analogies. In *Household and Community in the Mesoamerican Past,* ed. R. Wilk and W. Ashmore, pp. 135–151. Albuquerque: University of New Mexico Press.
  1991   *Household Ecology: Economic Change and Domestic Life among the Kekchi Maya in Belize.* Tucson: University of Arizona Press.

Wilk, R., and W. Ashmore
  1988   (Eds.) *Household and Community in the Mesoamerican Past.* Albuquerque: University of New Mexico Press.

Wilk, R., and W. Rathje
  1982   Household Archaeology. *American Behavioral Scientist* 25(6): 617–639.

Wilk, R., and H. Wilhite
  1991   The Community of Cuello: Patterns of Household and Settlement Change. In *Cuello: An Early Maya Community in Belize,* ed. N. Hammond, pp. 118–133. Cambridge: Cambridge University Press.

Willey, G.
  1956   (Ed.) *Prehistoric Settlement Patterns in the New World.* Viking Fund Publications in Anthropology, no. 23. New York: Wenner-Gren Foundation for Anthropological Research.
  1977   The Rise of Maya Civilization: A Summary View. In *The Origins of Maya Civilization,* ed. R. E. W. Adams, pp. 383–423. Albuquerque: University of New Mexico Press.

Willey, G., and R. Leventhal
  1979   Prehistoric Settlement at Copan. In *Maya Archaeology and Ethnohistory,* ed. N. Hammond and G. Willey, pp. 75–102. Austin: University of Texas Press.

Willey, G., R. Leventhal, and W. Fash
  1978   Maya Settlement in the Copan Valley. *Archaeology* 31(4): 32–43.

Willey, G., and J. Sabloff
  1980   *A History of American Archaeology.* San Francisco: Freeman.

Wisdom, C.
  1940   *The Chorti Indians of Guatemala.* Chicago: University of Chicago Press.

World Health Organization
  1989   *Health Principles of Housing.* Geneva.

Zalessky, B.
  1966   Use of Volcanic Tuffs and Tufflavas as Building Material. In *Tufflavas and Ignibrites—A Survey of Soviet Studies,* ed. E. Cook, pp. 197–200. New York: American Elsevier.

Zeledon, R., G. Solana, L. Burstin, and J. Swartzwelder
  1975   Epidemiological Patterns of Chagas' Disease in an Endemic Area of Costa Rica. *American Journal of Tropical Medicine and Hygiene* 24(2): 214–225.

Zhongshu, W.
  1982   *Han Civilization*. New Haven: Yale University Press.
Zhu, Z., and Z. Zhang
  1990   Maximum Acceptable Repetitive Lifting Workload by Chinese Subjects. *Ergonomics* 33(7): 875–884.

Index

(*Page references to tables and figures are set in italic type.*)